Reconstruction

of the Planetary Soul

Randi Green

Reconstruction

of the Planetary Soul

Reconstruction
of the Planetary Soul

Layout: Randi Green
ISBN 978-87-717059-4-2

Website
www.toveje.dk
The SETAH Initiative &
The Terra Transigo Academy

Other Books from the same Author
The Souls of Humanity
Terralogy
Understanding the Old Stellar Souls

Table of Contents

Introduction

The world we are part of is an artificial engineered world constructed to derail us from our true genetic composition and heritage. It is a world constructed to fit the needs and goals of foreign, to this planetary system, stellar races that came here to take part in programs aimed at helping and assisting these races. The planetary races, called LPRF1 humans, welcomed the stellar races, called LPRF2 humanoids, to this system with the intent of helping, teaching and assisting the stellar races in their regression and they paid back the hospitality with gratitude to begin with.

Many of the LPRF2 humanoids liked it here and chose to stay behind when the restoration program as such came to an end, or at least was downsized, due to issues in the LPRF2 systems. The era, when the LPRF2 humanoids and the LPRF1 humans collaborated, took place in the end days of Lemuria (the colonies of the 3rd and 4th planetary systems). In terms of memory recall, most of what we have access to transpired during the later period of the stellar Atlantis (the combined restoration and rehabilitation programs of the 4th and 5th planetary systems). However as we move along in the interplanetary story; that is the story of the 6 planetary systems and their main planets, called earths, it all changed when the Reptilian Riots began followed by the invasion of the infectious LPRF3s, which escaped their confinement in the dark light areas. The infected LPRF3s entered our system, using consciousness transfer[1] executed by the draco-reptilian

---

[1] Invocation is done by the use of symbols, energy and incantations to bridge the consciousness of the performer with the consciousness of the receiver. From this link it is possible to transfer genetics from one timeline to another. The performer of the invocation is then linked to the receiving consciousness and from there becomes the

overlords and their priests, as well as hostile regressed lizard groups, wanting more power including the sciences the infected LPRF3s still possessed. At that point in time the infected LPRF3s[2] were the only races left with the ancient memories and sciences of the far gone Sirian Workstations, the advanced levels of the genetic sciences from the first universe and the complete understanding of the LPU, the khundarays and so forth behind the LPRF2 systems: knowledge that would ensure the power and dominion of the draco-reptilians for eternity since they, with this knowledge, would be able to control, manipulate and rule over all the LPRF2 systems and the humanoids existing there.

This changed the collaboration between the stellar LPRF2s and the planetary LPRF1, which at that point in our planetary history had developed into a somewhat strained relationship due to the Templar Melchizedeks wanting more power too. It all ended with the taking over of our LPRF1 planetary system by the draco-reptilian overlords, the enslavement of the LPRF1 humans by the lizard landlords and their allied humanoid-human Templar Melchizedek (later called the LWBs) and the genetic modification of the LPRF1s.

The genetic modification enabled the foreign LOES (the level one energy system holding LPRF2 stellar genetics, i.e. the stellar soul) to attach to the modified and engineered LPRF1 human form (the newly engineered LPRF1 race after the takeover).

The foreign LOES were brought here from other LPRF2 systems, captured and sealed off while the original LPRF2 humanoid form was scattered to pieces with the goal of producing genetics, etc as part of a trade system created by the draco-reptilians. The genetic trade system advanced into an energetic production later on as the LPRF3s

---

host of the genetics of the receiver, integrating these into the energy system of the performer.

[2] Read the Appendix to understand the role LPRF3s have played in our system.

entered and the dark LPRF2s came to be due to their high level of infectious attached LPRF3 genetics. With this the astral barrier came to be.

All of this have been explained the previous three books.

In this book we work with the reconstruction of the planetary soul, the LPRF1 planetary energy system (the LPRF1 PES) holding the LPRF1 genetics, as it was created by the LPRF5s and the LPRF4s. To do this we need to know more and not the scarce glimpses we got in the three previous books, told through the filter of the LPRF2 humanoid memories. However we needed the stellar history to be able to choose how we want to continue in this system as a LPRF2 humanoid or a LPRF1 human.

If the LPRF2 LOES is integrated into the current human form, as it has been taught in the course Claiming Your Template, and the activated stellar personality decides to let go of the opportunity to leave and stay here, the LPRF2 LOES is transformed into the LPRF1 PES keeping the levels of the LPRF2 genetics that can be used to perform an advanced type of re-integration work as well as participate in the reconstruction work of our reality field on the LPRF1 and LPRF2 levels.

Begin the Purification Process
Sign up for the SETAH School on toveje.dk

1) You begin with *the SETAH Fundamentals*. Here you learn how to work with the chakra system and how to purify it as well as how to observe your mind and emotions, and in this learn to administer the energies these two faculties produce in you, adding more astral and mental energies to the chakra system.

2) Then you can move into the *SETAH Advanced,* working with your stellar soul or go to the Terra Transigo Academy *TTA Self-Study 1* where you work with the planetary soul.

The Future of our LPRF1 Planetary System

Overview of the terms from the Planetary Councils

a) By equinox 2017 the visiting stellar and galactic races (all LPRF2 humanoids and LPF3s) operating in our reality field have to have completed their host-field missions (part of the stellar activation cycle instigated by the crystalline LPRF2s and krystic LPRF3s), genetic extraction programs of bio-DNA (human DNA holds stellar genetics too) and stellar genetics in attached LOES, energy harvesting and similar activities, foreign to our system.[3]

b) Remaining LPRF2 humanoids operating from the LPRF2 network, such as the lizard LOES-human controllers, i.e. the elite and nobilities in charge of the monetary and political systems including all non-governmental projects operating to control this reality, as well as the avian-mammal LOES-human brotherhoods behind religious, spiritual and most scientific institutions, together forming the OWO, and other stellar factions present here, are sanctioned from further active use of the this system´s recourses and confined to the 4 racial timelines[4] under the control of the LPRF2 humanoids for now. The remaining LPRF2 humanoids are confined from further expansion and limited to the 4 racial timelines, using the LPRF2 network, to meet their need of time to unravel all genetic entanglement via networks inserted into the LPRF1 system. The goal with this is to enable them to leave.

---

[3] All viable and non-attached LPRF2 and LPRF3s are leaving around summer solstice 2016,. The rest will leave around winter solstice 2016. Specific portals are open around solstice. These portals will close down end 2016. With this a significant drop in energy will occur on our planet.

[4] Actually 5 racial timelines, but the NOA/NSEH have freely handed over their racial timeline to the Planetary Councils since they are more or less done with their work here. Hence only 4 are under the full control of the LPRF2s.

c) Negotiations with the crystalline LPRF2s and krystic LPRF3s, and other galactic races (false or dark light field) operating from the LPRF3 network, have agreed to let go of all claims on this LPRF1 system and accepted offerings enabling them to leave the LPRF1 system.

They have to leave in the years 2017-2025 the latest, although most of them will leave around solstice 2016, except from the crystalline LPRF2s collaborating with the krystic LPRF3s – they will stay behind completing their transhuman agendas with the LWBs. When they finally leave, they will hand over the LPRF3 network and the areas controlled by this[5] to the LPRF1 Planetary Councils.

d) The present planetary system (a merge of the 4th and 5th planetary systems, added with ancient features from the 3rd planetary system) will continue its resetting to be completed on a cosmic scale in 2065.

The resetting will be experienced as a slow progressing pole shift and accumulated changes in the current environment and structures.

The upper atmosphere and outer space will shift according to alterations in the spaceweather; for example unparalleled changes in the Sun cycles, higher levels of cosmic radiation, incoming celestial objects, etc as the Frequency Fence (a spectrum of frequencies controlling the planet and its humanity on an atomic level) is altered due to the ongoing projects and racial timeline decay.

e) The goal of the resetting is to reinstate Mars as the 5th planet[6] to sustain LPRF1 human life in the future. To obtain this, the 4th planet

---

[5] We are here talking about the direct control of areas by the galactic races, not the indirect control the LPRF3s have of the LPRF2 humanoids, being their "higher selves". The attached LPRF3s are confined by the same agreements as the remaining LPRF2s, they are attached to.
[6] In the years 2025-2065 Mars will sustain the LWBs and their Mars-Lunar projects functioning as the bridge into the crystalline LPRF2 parallel realities. After 2065 Mars and the Moon will be handed back to the Planetary Councils.

(Earth) will continue functioning as the main progression planet until the 5th and the 6th planetary systems can be recreated after 2065.

The future 6th planet will most likely unfold on Jupiter reviving the ancient levels of 6th planetary system coding in its gridwork, from the Sirian Workstations.

The three planetary systems are to express the lower, middle and upper LPRF1 areas as it is natural for a LPRF1 planetary system; i.e. the 4th planet will sustain the lowest progression levels and lifeforms, the 5th planet will unfold the middle progression levels and lifeforms, and the 6th planet will maintain the progression fields suitable for the LPRF1 humans of the upper areas.

f) The LPRF1 Planetary Councils and their operatives are to monitor and supervise the taken back LPRF1 system in the years to come as it resets from the upper to the lower reality fields, which means that the upper areas are to reset first followed by the middle areas. The lower and outer areas will not feel the positive changes before after 2025.

g) Original progression abilities are reinstated into the racial timelines under the administration of the LPRF1 Planetary Councils. The racial timelines are to operate under the gathered LPUs and their present day accepted progression rate, tied to the collaborating first Universe.

h) For now 8 out of the 12 racial timelines are under full control of the LPRF1 Planetary Councils. The remaining 4 racial timelines under the control of the LPRF2 human-humanoids are to be converted or let go off, if they cannot be restored.

For now 3 of the 4 racial timelines are estimated to go into full evaporation.

Access to the reinstated progression abilities

The remaining LPRF2 human-humanoid races with or without organic form, controlling our reality field and the world population serving under them, from hereon called the timeline collective, will only get access to the reinstated progression abilities if it is done by free will and by own effort.

The Planetary Councils will accept all 4th planetary present day humans and humanoids, willing to undergo the progression on an organic and energetic level, before the complete resetting.

The Timeline Collective (the remaining LPRF2 human-humanoids)

The OWO; that is the juxtaposing controllers and brotherhoods. They have the main genetic ownership of the world population as well as the full control of the LPRF2 network. However; they have outsourced shares of their ownership to the below groups as part of peace treaties, contracts, collaborations and trade opportunities.

− *The Pleiadian-Rostilians* have the genetic rights over the majority of the population in India, Asia and the access to the associated levels of the LPRF2 network.
− *The NOA/NSEH* has the genetic rights over the majority of humans in America and Canada, including sections of Britain and France,[7] except from the areas owned by the OWO. The NOA/NSEH utilizes an independent network, promoted by the Aryan-Shivas.
− *An unnamed ancient race of reptilians teaming up with the Grays*, unfolding their hybridization programs helped along by human operatives, parasiting on this system to rebuild their own. They

---

[7] Most of these areas are now under the crystalline LPRF2s collaborating with the OWO to ensure their continued existence. The NOA/NSEH has pulled out leaving their upgraded section of the timeline collective to the Planetary Councils. This section is positioned in the middle LPRF1 areas and thus not something we will notice for now. Only in terms of the LOES, the NOA/NSEH has left behind, do this matter.

are utilizing an ancient network type from the 3rd planetary system adapted to link up to the current merged planetary system.

- *The Nordics* have the genetic ownership of the majority in Russia, Eastern Europe except from the regions under the dominion of the Eastern Brotherhoods and their stellar allies of various races. The Nordics utilize an independent network connected to their home system as part of a host-mission.
- *The Orion Collective* has the genetic ownership of the population in China, parts of Mongolia and Asia. The Orion Collective utilizes an independent network connected to their home system using parallel system bridging with very little connection to this LPRF1 system. They are parasiting on this system to rebuild/sustain their own parallel systems.
- *The Maia-Pleiadians* have the genetic ownership of the population in Japan, Australia and parts of Asia, except from the areas under the OWO and the ancient reptilians similar to the ones found in America. They utilize a sector of the LPRF2 network specialized to draw upon the gridwork from the 3rd planetary system.
- *The Crystalline Sirian Bs*. They have the genetic ownership of the majority of South America, large parts of Scandinavia and Europe. They utilize parts of the LPRF3 network that extend into the LPRF2 network. The crystalline LPRF2s work together with the controllers and the brotherhoods in the ongoing projects, in spite of the competition between the controllers and brotherhoods.

As for now the current world population is seen as an intrinsic part of the timeline collective, engineered as they are to unfold this agenda, and they will stay under the control of the remaining LPRF2 races, cf. paragraph b. This means that our present world will stay under their jurisdiction for now.

The remaining LPRF2 human-humanoids are restricted to the racial timelines, they control and the future Mars-Lunar projects.

All LPRF2 and LPRF3 technologies are to be removed from the LPRF1 system. The removal begins in the upper, followed by the middle and completed into the lower areas following the other 8 timelines under the LPRF1 Planetary Councils. Mars will be the last planet to be cleared of the stellar technologies and races.

Restriction technologies have been inserted to the LPRF2 and LPRF3 networks preventing the remaining stellar and galactic races from exceeding the agreed terms of ongoing projects.

How does this affect us?
The outer areas and its humanity, as well as the inner areas and the LPRF2 human-humanoids exiting there, can at anytime begin the process of re-integration into the gathered LPUs. The process is available for all that are willing to participate in the reconstruction work to achieve the progression rate defined by the gathered LPUs. The re-integration process and the reconstruction work[8] run in phases until 2065, where the current LPRF1 system will have completed its resetting, if all goes after plan.

All remaining LPRF2 stellar humanoids with or without organic form, including active or dormant LOES, present in the 4th planetary system will after 2025 belong to this planetary system. It will be expected that they do a full re-integration process and take part in the reconstruction work of the 4th planetary system, and later on the 5th planetary system, living up to the standards of the gathered LPUs

---

[8] How to do this, is part of the Terra Transigo Academy self-study.

and their 5th evolutionary cycles.[9] All forms of gridworks and networks of the present LPRF1 system are in the process of being upgraded, transformed and altered to fit the present templars and energy systems of the gathered LPUs with the goal of reconnecting them to the collective of planetary systems. Only the secluded areas under the timeline collective will remain as they are until 2025. This means that the ongoing projects instigated by the timeline collective will not be interfered with other than the denial of further expansion upheld by the confinement, cf. paragraph b.

This means that the ongoing projects will continue in the years to come. The projects are part of the agreements made between the Planetary Councils and the remaining LPRF2 humanoids concerning the departure of the LPRF2 human-humanoids as soon as possible unless they agree to become part of the LPRF1 system, cf. the deadline of year 2025.

The Ongoing Projects
Projects focused on upgrading the bio-DNA to higher conductivity
The intensification of the Frequency Fence run by the controllers and their LPRF2 LWBs and human affiliates (working with both secret and known programs funded by private contractors, non-governmental organizations and institutions) will continue. These projects have the goal to change the adult segment of the world's population, enabling

---

[9] Which explains the hurry the LPRF2 humanoids were in, which I felt whenever I was in contact with them. All the time when I worked my way through the LPRF2 network in the purification process, I had this immanent feeling of having to hurry because the end was near. Well, it was not the end of our planet per se but the end for the racial timelines under their control, the LPRF2 network as well as the completion of the timeline loops. Naturally the present racial timelines are decaying, which kind of put an end to any future projects here, but also because the LPRF2s had already gotten the message of leaving. They got this around 2009 from the LPRF1 Planetary Councils. I was not able to perceive this until I shifted from my humanoid LOES to my LPRF1 PES, cf. my combined human-humanoid energy system from the stellar Atlantis.

them to bring into being new genetic alterations in the forthcoming generations of humanity.[10]

The amplifying is aimed at raising the conductivity of the human cells by adding high amounts of targeted chemical compounds known for their capability to be electrically charged. When absorbed into the human body, the cells will adapt to the exposure of the chemical compounds[11] and respond to the intensified frequencies run through the Frequency Fence, enabling an increased level of extreme low frequencies (ELF) to permeate the membrane of the cells.

The intensification of the Frequency Fence is done by the use of frequency technologies on many levels. Underground facilities with high-energy particle accelerators such as CERN and LHC as well as the German DESY, to name a few,[12] affect the core quantum fields and the connection between humans and the planetary emission fields.

Low-ground wireless technology (tablets, iPhone etc), LED, blue light technologies and ELF towers have an effect on the lower levels of the geomagnetic field interacting with and upholding the human bio-electromagnetic field targeting the electric circuits of the cells, such as the heart, the central nervous system and effectiveness of the brain.[13] High-ground facilities such as HAARP[14] and other forms of ELF

---

[10] Changes in one generation ensure long term changes in the overall population.

[11] We are here talking about the epigenetics, where the non-coding RNA is activated to ignite what genes that are suppressed and which are not. The goal is to produce a resilient and frequency adjustable bio-DNA similar to the dimensional frequencies found in newer and artificial LPRF2 stellar systems. Read about epigenetics here: http://www.whatisepigenetics.com/fundamentals/

[12] List of high-energy particle accelerators worldwide:
https://en.wikipedia.org/wiki/List_of_accelerators_in_particle_physics

[13] Which means that the core of the chakras are affected as well, making them more receptible to higher dimensional energies from the platforms the LPRF2s want to link up to, i.e. the "ascension of humanity", where all are to become 5th dimensionals. A truth with many modifications and false promises.

[14] On HAARP; the Stanford VLF Group: http://vlf.stanford.edu/research/experiments-haarp-ionospheric-heater

and VLF technologies, satellites and high altitude equipment have an impact on the ionosphere in conjunction with weather modification programs (white chemtrails). These programs are aimed at affecting the collective mind field, i.e. the emission field generated by the total sum of energetic processes, unfolded in the brains of the population of the world and from there go into the core of the bio-DNA affecting the electromagnetic emission field of the human body and in this alter the molecular structure in humanity. Additional programs, to support the frequency technologies, such as GMO and chemical enriched foods are produced to alter the pH value in the body, making the glands, the electro-chemical levels in the cells and the periphery nervous system respond to the frequency technologies.

These projects will not be disrupted in spite of the affects they have on the environment and the high fatality rate as well as a lower fertility rate in all species. The understanding is that the current world population is part of the genetic ownership of the controllers and as such they decide what is best for the engineered forms and what they are to evolve into.[15]

Projects on alteration of the human bio-DNA into new sequences
The hybrid, trans- and superhuman projects run by the controllers and their human affiliates (MILABS and similar forms of clandestine military-scientific operations) and other collaborating factions of the timeline collective will continue the projects aimed at the younger and unborn generations.

These projects involve abductions, unauthorized experiments and hidden sciences for example air-born viral programs (dark chemtrails) affecting mothers to be and their yet to be born children, as well as mothers in progress carrying unborn children, with nano-genetic

---

[15] Humans respond differently to these programs; some will evolve into the wanted frequency spectrum in cells and consciousness, whereas others will develop diseases.

technology[16] using bacterial and dormant viral carriers[17] from known diseases[18] or new carriers, cf. the zika virus and the like, to execute genetic mutations that will lead to a human 2.0 prototype.

The early stages of the nano-genetic experiments were part of the vaccination programs but as the awareness rose in humanity, the experiments have been abandoned. The sciences have developed since then and there is no further need for direct injections. The plus side is that many concerned parents are now avoiding the vaccination programs thinking they are protecting their offspring, when they in fact are exposing them to ancient and new types of viruses used in the air-born viral programs. Thus many forms of old and new diseases will rise in youngsters making them more receptible to the air-born viruses, leading to genetic mutations.

These programs have the goal of altering the present bio-DNA to be able to link up to stellar technologies placed in the 4th dimension (to some degree also the 5th) using the LPRF2 network to execute this work in this reality. From here new types of bio-DNA will unfold (three base pairs as well as triple DNA helices) and by this enable the remaining LPRF2 stellar races to get out using the hybrid, trans- or superhuman bio-system and its adapted LOES.[19]

---

[16] The substance and coloration in the dark chemtrails stem from carbon nanotubes: https://en.wikipedia.org/wiki/Fullerene

[17] Read about viruses: https://en.wikipedia.org/wiki/Virus

[18] A typical carrier would be an emptied out HIV virus or viruses from the plague, where the virus itself has been modified and now works as a carrier for the nano-genetic content. These viruses are highly adaptable and are easily absorbed into the cells, where the carrier releases its content altering the cellular structure, also known as mutation of genes.

[19] Quite a lot of the work done with the LOES is done during nighttime, where the LOES attached to the human body undergoes modification including alterations on the chakra system from early childhood. The Gray-reptilian-human hybrid programs, i.e. Novo Sapiens are a fine example but also unknowing humans are part of these programs.

The programs will not be will not be disrupted in spite of the high mortality rate in children and youngsters (dropping dead suddenly by hidden organic failure), including the unwanted side effects such as ADHD, autism and other forms of neurological diseases (weird pains in the limbs, spasms, etc), which are part of the adjustment process of the human biology.

Read more about the sciences supporting the ongoing projects. The scientists promoting the experiments are programmed (chakra system control) to make the technologies in the hidden projects public:

- *Optogenetics: Controlling the Brain with Light*
  http://www.scientificamerican.com/article/optogenetics-controlling/

- *Optogenetics: Controlling Cell Function with Light*
  http://www.nature.com/nmeth/journal/v8/n1/full/nmeth.f.323.html

- *Scientists discover that our brain waves can be sent by electrical fields*
  http://www.sciencealert.com/scientists-discover-new-method-of-brain-wave-transmission-electrical-fields

- *Physicists prove energy input predicts molecular behavior*
  http://phys.org/news/2016-03-physicists-energy-molecular-behavior.html

- *Scientists create new nanotech building blocks*
  https://biodesign.asu.edu/news/scientists-create-new-nanotech-building-blocks

- *Peptide nucleic acid (PNA): its medical and biotechnical applications and promise for the future* http://www.fasebj.org/content/14/9/1041.full

- *DNA Triple Helices: biological consequences and therapeutic potential*
  http://www.ncbi.nlm.nih.gov/pmc/articles/PMC2586808/

- *A new glycerol nucleic acid (GNA) building block for structural DNA nanotechnology* https://www.foresight.org/nanodot/?p=2728

The LPU and the Planetary Systems

The LPRF1 system we are part of is much more complicated than the restricted level of perception, we are engineered to have.

To understand the 6 planetary systems, which have unfolded known lifeforms in our solar system, i.e. the LPRF1 system,[20] we have to understand the construction of the less progressive universe (the LPU) we are part of. The LPU consists of 5 less progressive reality fields (LPRFs).

Our LPU

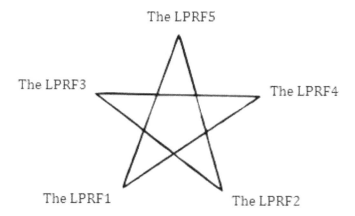

---

[20] It is more correct to call our solar system a planetary system (the LPRF1 system in total) since the star in our solar system was dragged here when the draco-reptilians, or perhaps some older stellar races, wanted to generate an environment similar to a stellar system in our system. In a stellar system the stars are the manifested areas, into which the holographic stellar races unfold their forms.

When the Progenitors, i.e. the elder human-humanoids from the first universe, decided to create our LPU, they began with their own level.

Due to their level of development unfolded in the 5th evolutionary cycle of the first universe, they elevated to a higher level, once they entered the 4th evolutionary cycle and thus became the LPRF5s.

As you might remember from *Understanding the Old Stellar Souls*: *The soul groups integrate as soul races into the evolutionary cycles of which there are six. Each evolutionary cycle overlaps the previous, which means that there is a point, where a cycle is unfolding as a pure cycle and then there are two stages, where a cycle unfolds as a mixed one leaving a cycle and as a mixed one entering the next cycle.*

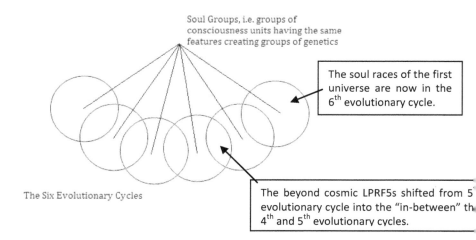

Soul Groups, i.e. groups of consciousness units having the same features creating groups of genetics

The soul races of the first universe are now in the 6th evolutionary cycle.

The Six Evolutionary Cycles

The beyond cosmic LPRF5s shifted from 5 evolutionary cycle into the "in-between" the 4th and 5th evolutionary cycles.

The Creation of the LPU

The LPRF5s have been called many names: the highest spheres of consciousness, the monads, the eternal consciousness, the assembly of divine powers, the first true existence and analogous expressions found all over the world rooting back to the time, when humanity still got glimpses of the entities that created the LPU, i.e. the cosmos we are part of. As the elder human-humanoids entered the levels that turned into the LPU, they gave up having a human-humanoid form. Instead they became raw consciousness units generating the all prevailing fields of consciousness that lie beneath the entire LPU.

The LPRF5 consciousness units are called *the Keys of Ascension*, because the one that enters the true heaven will get the keys to the kingdom, to use a Christian idiom, and from there know what needs to be done to truly collaborate with the LPRF5s using the integrated consciousness units, now part of the human or humanoid energy system. From that point on the human or humanoid becomes a conscious member of the LPU and the consciousness fields upholding all that there is in it.

When the LPRF5s had spread out as raw consciousness fields and encompassed the areas, they wanted to cover as their reality fields, called the less progressive reality fields (the LPRFs), they began the second level of creation, which was the stellar LPRF2 realities. Here they created holographic-particle forms suitable for the humanoid genetics, they had brought with them from the first universe.[21]

The stellar LPRF2 systems were created similar to the realities the humanoid genetics were accustomed to in the first universe albeit accommodated to the in between cycles type of holographic units.

Then the Progenitors, another name for the LPRF5s, created an overseeing race to take care of the development of the LPRF2s, which needed help to progress. The overseers became the galactic LPRF3s. These races existed as light beings, in our interpretation of things, albeit they are more correctly to be seen as sound-light entities unfolding their genetics as light-strands of consciousness within the tonal-wave (sound and light) scalar fields. From there the Progenitors

---

[21] Again read the Appendix to get a better understanding. I keep that history there since this section is focused on the LPRF1 reality perception and not the LPRF2 humanoid, reflected in the Appendix.

kept their promises to the cosmic forces that existed in the in between cycles, i.e. the LPRF4s. The LPRF4s were trapped in the 4th evolutionary cycle as forces. Since the soul genetics had shifted into the 5th evolutionary cycle, leaving the realities of the 4th cycle behind, the energetic units of the 4th cycle were left to burn out on their own, and as the Progenitors returned, the forces got a second chance to develop as energy connected to a consciousness principle. They were given form as nebulae or cosmic fields from which they could interact with the raw consciousness of the Progenitors, generating what we could call the highest forces; i.e. the Hebrew Elohim. As such the Elohim became the manifested expression of the Progenitors on a lower level.

The Elohim-LPRF4s and the galactic-LPRF3s worked as a unit with structuring and transforming of the energies of the 4th evolutionary cycle into 5th evolutionary cycle holographic units on the tonal-wave planes, laying the foundation of the Sirian Workstations.

The galactic-LPRF3s instigated experiments using the holographic forces, and from this they produced the lower areas of the Sirian Workstations expanding the LPRF3 realities into the LPRF2 systems, giving grounds for the LPRF3 network in the LPRF2 gridwork.

The last creation of the Progenitors was the LPRF1 planetary level. This level was created as a pure LPU type of reality using the LPRF4 cosmic forces and the LPRF5 raw consciousness units to generate a LPRF1 human unfolded as particle beings, specialized in transforming the LPRF4 forces by invoking the LPRF5 consciousness units within on the most basic levels.

Because the LPRF1 planetary races were the last to be created and due to their long progression journey, from the LPRF1, to the LPRF2, to the LPRF3 etc., they were installed with what could be called unique progression abilities, able to transform into holographic and tonal-wave properties. In each of the consciousness layers of the

LPRF1 planetary energy system, using the LPRF1 particle or human form, the genetics of the LPRF1, the LPRF2 and the LPRF3s would transform the forces of the LPRF4 and the raw consciousness units from the LPRF5s, symbiotically merged into the LPRF1 human form.

As the LPRF1 humans progressed, working with the energies they were composed of, the raw consciousness units would grow and expand, and from there break through the LPRF4 forces, while the LPRF1 human form was still in the planetary system.

The planetary human was intrinsically linked to the energy system of the LPRF1 system, i.e. the planetary templar with the goal of developing as many timelines of the templar as possible, being part of the energy transforming mission, the LPRF1 humans were created to perform.[22]

Therefore; only if 8 out of the 12 racial timelines - and their LPRF1 type of consciousness genetics - were developed by the LPRF1 humans and transformed through the inbuilt LPRF4 forces, i.e. the particle units the planetary system and the LPRF1 human form were generated of, could the LPRF1 planetary energy system, i.e. LPRF1 soul, leave and go back to the first universe or, if preferred, continue in the LPU as a LPRF2 or LPRF3 entity.

With this the six planetary systems are easier to comprehend with this in mind, given that each of the planetary systems, their main planets and version of the LPRF1 planetary humans were to reflect the transformational stage of the LPRF4s energies and the inbuilt LPRF5 consciousness units, the LPRF1 humans were created of, and the levels they had to progress through to develop the planetary templar and the khundarays in the gridwork, expressed as different types of reality possibilities.

---

[22] The LPRF2s were created to upgrade and evolve their first universe less developed genetics. The LPRF3s were created to build reality fields and oversee the LPRF2s and LPRF1s to some extent. All had their place and missions in the LPU.

The LPRF1 Planetary Systems and Root Races

The 1st planetary system and its races were composed of a type of LPRF5-LPRF4-LPRF1, i.e. as combinations of raw-units-cosmic-force-particle energies and LPRF1 consciousness. The 1st root race[23] was connected to the LPRF4s and the LPRF5s building the ground of the LPRF1 planetary system in "the likeness and image" of the LPRF4s, meaning that they unfolded the first merged version of the LPRF4s and the LPRF5s into a raw particle form similar to what we could call a type of core beings.

The 1st root race did not exist for long for the reason that they were an intermediary race, although their memories and experiences are an intrinsic part of the core of our planetary system, vibrating there as fields of the first type of consciousness in this system. The Hebrew Bible and the Apocrypha refer to the initial LPRF1 humans as the first creation of the Elohim existing in the Gan Eden walking among the angels, or as some other writers place them; as the angels themselves. The first races and the LPRF4s built the entire foundation of the LPRF1 planetary system.

The 1st root race changed into the 2nd root race, forming the 2nd planetary system called Inner Earth. These areas still exist in our planetary reality fields as part of the upper LPRF1 areas, although the current 2nd root race have changed into a type that is more similar to the 3rd root race.

The 2nd root race worked via a combination of LPRF5-LPRF3-LPRF1, i.e. raw-units-tonal-wave-particle energies and LPRF1 consciousness and existed in the highest vibrating levels of the upper LPRF1 areas, unfolding the next stage of the planetary gridwork. They pulled in the khundarays of the LPU to our system, with the goal of evolving the

---

[23] It is called a root race because they are the race founding a planetary system, as in laying the foundation of that specific system. Later races developed from the root races; however these secondary races do not have the same level of importance, since they are combinations of the root races.

LPRF4 forces. Again the raw consciousness units played a pivoted role, transforming the Elohim-LPRF4s forces and the khundarays of the highest level of the upper LPRF1 areas by the use of the tonal-wave LPRF3 genetic strands unfolded as part of a sound-light-particle transparent form, if we were to understand the type of body, they had.

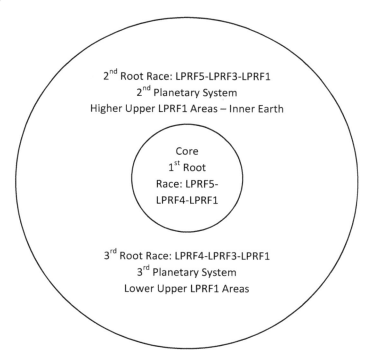

The 3rd root race progressed via a combination of LPRF4-LPRF3-LPRF1, i.e. as force-tonal-wave-particle energies and LPRF1 consciousness. They existed in the lower levels of the upper LPRF1 areas (the upper LPRF1 areas are divided into two sections), unfolding the third stage of the planetary gridwork. The 3rd root race unfolded LPRF4 energy units as an intrinsic part of their LPRF1 body in a very tall and slim type of form, highly receptible to changes instigated by the LPRF3 type of consciousness, developed by the 2nd root race.

In the end times of the 3rd root race, the timeline event occurred (I have earlier put this at the end of the 2nd root race, but today I think it was at the end of the 3rd root race). This altered the tonal-wave properties of the LPRF3 systems, generating fragmented frequencies, i.e. the frequency spectrum. The LPRF3 races, unfolding this type of energy and consciousness, were hit by the infection. It also affected our planetary system, producing new forms of energies as well as the inner and outer manifestation fields, which our planetary system has been forced to develop to extremes due to the astral barrier.

The 3rd root race and the 3rd planetary system; called Lemuria[24] or the Colonies, was highly affected by the timeline event and generated a whole new type of energies forcing the 4th root race to occur before the 3rd had completed their transformation work. This compelled the first three planetary systems, united as a whole, to become part of the next three planetary systems in a way that had not been foreseen by the LPRF5s.

Due to the repulsion barrier between the LPRF4 and the LPRF3 levels[25] the LPRF5s and the LPRF4s lost contact with the systems below the repulsion barrier. All that was left in our system from these levels were the merged LPRF4-LPRF5 energy-consciousness fields that had already been laid into the LPRF1 planetary gridwork.

As for the rest of the systems below the repulsion barrier, the LPRF3s were secluded and quarantined in the dark areas, i.e. the infected light areas. The LPRF2s lost contact with the Progenitors and got stuck with the small units of consciousness of the Progenitors had laid into the LPRF2 realities to begin with, through the khundarays. The remaining connection was totally lost as the regression kicked in

---

[24] Not to be confused with the continent of Mu found on the Internet.

[25] The repulsion barrier is explained in *the Souls of Humanity* and *Terralogy*.

and took over the stellar humanoids, forcing them to rely on complex technologies for all further progression.[26]

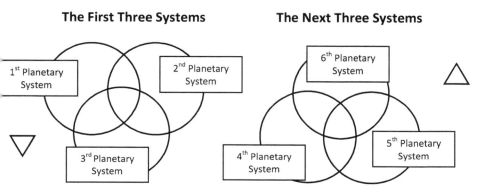

The First Three Systems   **The Next Three Systems**

The 4th planetary system was called Panergeia and unfolded in the middle LPRF1 levels laying the foundation of our current earth planet full of animals and plants. The plants and animals had very little similarity to the plants and animals, we know of today, because they were composed of the same type of energies and consciousness as the 4th root race, and to a high extent they were the 4th root race.

The 4th root race progressed via a LPRF4-LPRF2-LPRF1 combination of force-holographic-particle energies and LPRF1 consciousness.

The 4th root race exist today as part of the middle LPRF1 areas but have been secluded as the LPRF2 stellar humanoids took over a huge section of the middle LPRF1 areas, utilizing the LPRF2 network[27] to adapt sectors of the middle LPRF1 areas into a stellar holographic-particle type of reality called the 4th dimension by most, from which the astral barrier and astral plane unfolds. The 4th root race appear to us as human-like shapes resembling present day humanity (they laid

---

[26] Go to the Appendix to get a more complete story here.
[27] The LPRF2 network developed as part of the restoration programs.

the foundation of the human form), called the Asuras[28] or Deva and Devi (Suras)[29] in the Vedas. Due to their strong human similarity, they are not the same as the LPRF3 fragment infused astral entities, known in the new age teachings as devas, nature spirits, fairies, angels etc.[30]

To return to our true LPRF1 human consciousness and progression abilities, our reconstruction work and consciousness progression has to reconnect to the 4th root race in the middle LPRF1 areas, which is only possible when we have integrated and transformed the LPRF2 LOES, understanding that the LOES is not our natural middle LPRF1 level of consciousness. The LPRF2 LOES leads us to the LPRF2 network (or the false light fields of the LPRF3 network, if we have genetics enabling us to develop strands in the vortexes) preventing us from accessing the true LPRF1 middle areas. When we reconnect to the suras (deva-devi)[31], we regain access to the middle LPRF1 areas of our planetary system. This work goes through the present human form, which we will learn about later on.

The 5th planetary system is called the stellar Atlantis to distinguish it from Plato´s earthly Atlantis. It unfolded in the middle LPRF1 levels closest to the lower LPRF1 areas and held the 5th root race.

The 5th root race was not natural to our LPRF1 system, but was created as part of the restoration programs inviting existing LPRF2 humanoids to our planetary system to heal and assist them from the aftermath of the timeline event as an attempt to circumvent the regression.

---

[28] Asura – negative being - Wikipedia: https://en.wikipedia.org/wiki/Asura
[29] Devas/Suras Wikipedia: https://en.wikipedia.org/wiki/Deva_(Hinduism) meaning "heavenly, divine, terrestrial things of high excellence, exalted, shining ones."
[30] We only get a glimpse of their true properties in the works of Alice A. Bailey and how they influence present day humanity.
[31] Gender became part of the 4th root race due to the timeline event and the division of Sirian A and Sirian B consciousness traits.

The 5th root race unfolded as a LPRF3-LPRF2-LPRF1 combination of tonal-wave-holographic-particle energies and LPRF1-LPRF2 combined consciousness to meet up with the requirements of the restoration program.

The Templar Melchizedek human-humanoids came to be in the 5th planetary system. It is also in the 5th planetary system *the Souls of Humanity, Terralogy* and *Understanding the Old Stellar Souls* unfold, leading to present day combined 4th and 5th planetary-solar system after the Sun was brought here from a destroyed reptilian-mammal LPRF2 stellar system, enabling the draco-reptilians and the later new stellar races to exist here.

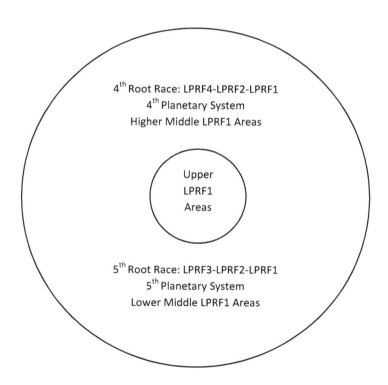

4th Root Race: LPRF4-LPRF2-LPRF1
4th Planetary System
Higher Middle LPRF1 Areas

Upper
LPRF1
Areas

5th Root Race: LPRF3-LPRF2-LPRF1
5th Planetary System
Lower Middle LPRF1 Areas

The LPRF3 network is placed a bit higher than the LPRF2 network and was not fully unfolded until after the invocation of the highest LPRF3s which created the false light field, i.e. a type of holographic-wave type of reality, using the LPRF3 network and the mental plane to exist here. The false light field is positioned in the 5th dimension and is controlled by the crystalline LPRF2s and the krystic LPRF3s.

The Present LPRF1 Gridwork and the Manifested Areas

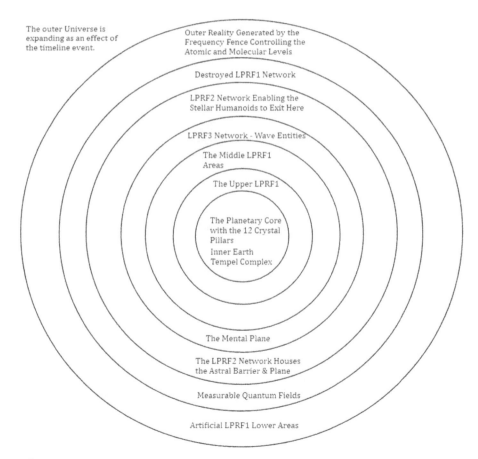

Inner reality controls the outer reality ("from above")

Distorted light fields merged into the holographic fields, unfolded as
a) Highest level of the middle LPRF1 areas changed using the LPRF3 network. This area is the plane of existence for the highest LPRF3s, called *the false light field*. The highest are bright cold light beings that reverse all light units of whoever comes in contact with them. Also called *the higher mental plane*.
b) The lower level of the middle LPRF1 areas have been changed by the use of the LPRF2 network into semi-holographic planes called *the lower mental and astral planes*. They are the planes of existence for the lesser functional LPRF3s (incl. higher devas) in our reality field, as well as the LPRF2 dark ones (called this due to their dark light field). The LWBs that to a high degree are dark ones themselves, exit there as well.
c) Upper levels of the lower LPRF1 areas, changed by the use of the ancient technologies behind the crystal pillars, altered into a construction called *the astral barrier*, controlling the psychological level of the human population by determining the outcome of the subtle energies producing electrochemical reactions (emotions and thoughts) via the chakra system behind the atomic form.

Outer reality is controlled from "above and below"
Manifested molecular physical reality, biology and higher lifeforms.
- From above via the chakra system controlling the minds of biological forms.
- From below via the Frequency Fence, aka frequency control of the cells.

Deeper reality controls the outer reality ("from below")
Energetic levels, science can see unfolded as
a) Atomic level.
b) Sub-atomic levels.
c) Quantum levels (the visible level of the CQFs).

The geomagnetic field
aka the Frequency Fence
(LPRF3 controlled)

Core Quantum Fields (CQFs), science cannot see unfolded as
a) 1st Core quantum field with slightly changed LPRF1 particles.
b) 2nd Core quantum field with LPRF1-LPRF2 holographic units.
c) 3rd Core quantum field with LPRF1-LPRF3 tonal-wave units.

The Outer and Inner LPRF1 Areas

To begin the reconstruction work, we need a firm understanding of our manifestation field as it is today. Since I have already spent three books explaining the LPRF2 and LPRF3 networks and their manifested inner counterparts; that is the 4th and 5th artificial dimensions (a term used when the talk is about artificially generated planes of existence) as well as their participation in the outer realities as souls behind the bloodlines (controllers) or brotherhoods in human form (LWBs), I will not offer much attention to them here, except that the networks are the non-solidified energetic areas where the stellar and galactic races can exist as energy systems, i.e. souls if you like, as part of our reality field.

The outer Universe is expanding as an effect of the timeline event.

Outer Reality Generated by the Frequency Fence Controlling the Atomic and Molecular Levels

Destroyed LPRF1 Network

LPRF2 Network Enabling the Stellar Humanoids to Exit Here

LPRF3 Network - Wave Entities

The Middle LPRF1 Areas

The Upper LPRF1

The Planetary Core with the 12 Crystal Pillars
Inner Earth Tempel Complex

The Mental Plane

The LPRF2 Network Houses the Astral Barrier & Plane

Measurable Quantum Fields

Artificial LPRF1 Lower Areas

The artificial 4th and 5th dimensions enable them to take on energetic holographic-particle forms using the energies humans have generated being linked up to the astral and mental planes. The total planetary field consists of 12 timelines and 12 different energetic sections, pieced together into the LPRF1 planetary system.

I have illustrated the areas of the planetary system in concentric circles but they are more to be seen as areas in a unified large LPRF1 field, divided by energetic difference in non-solidified energy systems and LPU genetics, i.e. consciousness compositions. This means that stellar humanoids and their essences are positioned in specific areas, manifested using the four timeline and their corresponding energetic areas as part of the LPRF2-LPRF3 networks. These areas are then used to exist here and from there "incarnate" or take on solidified form in the outer areas, merging with the latest human prototype they have created some 4,500 years ago to be able to hold the stellar genetics. These areas exist side by side with the planetary non-solidified energy systems and LPU genetics, i.e. their consciousness compositions and their areas, although the stellar and planetary souls are not in direct contact with each other in the inner realities.[32]

The rules of affinity apply to a large degree to the "spirit world", to use the typical expression regarding the inner reality fields and their energetic features. This means that only the same type of energy systems and consciousness works together, dividing the inner world into sections reflecting the energy systems and their consciousness compositions (LPU soul genetics). The "spirit world" is not a world for spirits. It is a world of inner energetic areas, i.e. our planetary reality field as it looked before the time line event. The inner worlds and

---

[32] This is confirmed by the soul testimonies from the books *Journey of Souls* (1994) and *Destiny of Souls* (2000) by Michael Newton. I use his books to get the direct testimonies from the planetary souls, i.e. the non-solidified humans of the different root races exiting in the inner realities.

their lifeforms unfold as non-solidified energy systems in all aspects of the LPU, the gathered LPUs (the G-LPUs) and the first universe.

These non-solidified energy systems and their many consciousness compositions use another type of energy dissimilar to the outer molecular organic forms and thus we see them as "souls" or energetic beings. The outer organic features we find in all aspects of the after timeline event LPU came as a result of the solidification process, meaning that before the timeline event there were no organic forms as we know them; there were only various types of energetic systems composed of the LPRF5-LPRF1 field energies as explained earlier.

Before the timeline event the non-solidified energy systems and their consciousness compositions were the natural form to all of the races in the LPU and the first universe and subsequently, the later G-LPU. Due to the manifested outer areas, this changed adding a new type of form into which the energy systems and their consciousness compositions (soul genetics) could merge and from that develop in new directions.

We tend to see the non-solidified humans and humanoids of any reality field as the "souls" being part of a spirit world. The fact is that the energy systems are the manifestation form of the soul genetics. The soul in our understanding[33] is thus not the non-solidified energy systems most misinterpret to be souls, but the soul genetics of which the energy system is composed.

The soul genetics, whether it is the LPU genetics or the soul genetics of the first universe, are the part that is linked to the Source Cycles. Our LPU genetics are, via the consciousness genetics of the Progenitors in all reality fields of the LPU, linked to the Source Cycles of the first universe, so we are not severed from the true Source.

---

[33] Here I refer to our understanding as in the piece that is part of the Source cycles and subsequently the LPU.

The error humans in solidified forms do is that they only see the non-solidified energy systems, i.e. the forms that the inner world is using to develop the soul genetics, and in this they interpret these to be the souls that are linked up to Source (a the god-head); however the non-solidified forms are just as dispensable and changeable as the molecular form.

This means that there is no "spirit world" but an inner world, where the soul races of the LPU develop their soul genetics, using the non-solidified energy systems to be able to exist in the different sections of the planetary system. When the soul genetics, whether it is LPU or first universe genetics, change and mature the non-solidified energy system changes along with this, pulling - by the laws of affinity - the non-solidified energy system and its soul genetics to the area that is in energetic and consciousness likeness with the non-solidified energy system.

Most of the LPRF2 and LPRF1 non-solidified energy systems with their consciousness compositions go into the outer areas, from time to time, where they develop their genetics in organic or solidified forms as part of the progression, they wish to take on to themselves, but also to fulfill the purpose of their reality field.

In viewing things like this I specifically talk about the races that are collaborating with the first universe, and in this are trying to dissolve and transmute the outer areas back into the same state as the inner areas, completing the cycles of progression and evolution they began as part of the LPU but also as part of the first universe.

The G-LPUs and the first universe work together in resetting the effects of the timeline event, as well as the effects of the Internal Strife that took place eons ago in the first universe. It all comes down to the acknowledgement that things are as they are now, and what we can do to keep up the progression rate of all systems, whether they are part of the G-LPUs or the first universe.[34] Let us proceed into the understanding of the outer areas and their divisions into:

1. Physical, i.e. atomic and molecular.
2. Quantum, i.e. the destroyed LPRF1 network.
3. Astral, i.e. the energetic band created by human emotions and the subconscious.
4. Mental, i.e. the artificial energetic band created by human thought forms and ideas, acting as the collective human consciousness field.

We have to remember that these levels are only visible and accessible for the human psyche and mind because they are our creations. This means that only if we incarnate into the outer areas is it possible to work with these manifestation fields and transform them as well.

The Frequency Fence or Geomagnetic Field
There is not much to add to the information on the Frequency Fence and the geomagnetic field[35]; suffice to say is that further information

---

[34] Of course the LPRF2 races with their attached infected LPRF3 clusters, including the most regressed LPRF2s are counteracting this program of progression, which we know of in our system. The testimonies from the clients of Michael Newton do not go into this problem; they barely scratch the surface, avoiding answering this with "this is not part of our areas". The issues with the humans on this planet are not addressed in his books because it was not the time to give this information, when his books were written. They were completed in 2000 just around the time when the stellar factions, having been invited here as energy systems (non-solidified inner forms) to participate in the outer and inner 5th root races and stellar Atlantis. In 2000 the human-humanoids began their last chance of taking over our planetary system in full, but failed, cf. the Future of Our Planetary System where we learn of their departure out of our reality field, on both the inner and outer levels in 2017-2025. In other words; as the LPRF3 and LPRF2 networks are closed down, they cannot manifest in the outer human world, nor take part of the inner non-solidified levels of our reality field.

regarding the geomagnetic field can be found on the Internet and in *the Souls of Humanity*, where I touch the origin of the geomagnetic field. Naturally the Frequency Fence did not exist to begin with. It was incorporated later on into the magnetic flow of the outer planetary field, generating a sort of control mechanism limiting the atomic level of our reality by keeping the frequencies in a specific spectrum.

The Frequency Fence is linked to the astral barrier and since the astral barrier is dissolving due to the dissolving crystals in the four timelines related to our part of the planetary system, the Frequency Fence dismantles too, hence the invention of the new technologies to adjust and control the atomic level, as well as the electrochemical and electric currents in the human body, cf. the ongoing projects.[36]

The Leylines

Leylines are the natural energy lines of the original magnetic field of the planet that arose after the timeline event. They differ from the geomagnetic lines due to their ability to be programmed through the crystals in the core of our planet.

The leylines run the energies, infused into the planet from the core crystals,[37] on what we could call a chakra level in the planetary morphogenetic field (the PMF, i.e. the blueprint of the 4th planetary system), controlling the set up of the original energetic level in the PMF; however these lines of energy and their gathering into nodal points have been strongly manipulated since the takeover and thus the original set up from the crystal pillars are long gone, at least in the outer version of the leylines.

Today they are the intersection point between the astral barrier (holographic-wave technology controlling the production of the astral

---

[35] Also watch the video I have on the Planetary Update YouTube Channel about the geomagnetic field.
[36] Go to the Future of Our Reality to understand this.
[37] Both the pre-timeline event set of crystals and the post-timeline event sets.

and mental planes) and the Frequency Fence (controlling the atomic and molecular levels), grounding it into the natural magnetic field of the planet. Leylines and the chakra system in humans were set up to interconnect through the perception field programming (the astral barrier).

The Molecular Plane and Its Form

The molecular body is the present outer human prototype and was reengineered around 4,500 years ago as the astral barrier was put in place. It has been modified since to fit the different agendas of the timeline collective and is to this day being modified on all levels, cf. the ongoing programs.

The outer form is under the control of the timeline collective and yet the planetary souls (the non-solidified original root races) use these to enter the outer areas. The outer forms of the root races, which existed before the takeover, do not exist anymore in these four timelines and hence the planetary souls, living as part of the non-controlled areas, i.e. the other 8 timelines in our system, use the current engineered forms.

The original non-solidified root races see no problems in that since they only use around 20% of the total sum of human bodies to work here. Plus the planetary souls work here incognito, so to speak, without remembering who and what they are; hence the timeline collective do not see them as a threat to their agendas here.

From the perspective of the Planetary Councils and the inner root races, it poses no problem to them that the outer form is controlled by the timeline collective, or the type of world the timeline collective has created, because they know it is a temporary setting (a bump in the road) and that things will eventually return to "normal", cf. the end of the reign of the draco-reptilians, the controllers and the present timeline collective.[38] Besides, from the standpoint of the planetary souls the world and their human forms under the timeline collective is an intriguing form to learn to control and master. It gives variations to the consciousness compositions.[39]

The molecular body, i.e. the outer form suitable to exist in the outer areas, is used by galactic, stellar and planetary non-solidified energy systems for various purposes in the four manifested timelines of our system. The different non-solidified energy systems merge with the outer form to be able to work here. It is only possible to work in the outer areas, if the inner energy systems have merged directly with an outer form. Only then is it possible to do any work of transformation (changing the features of the outer energies) or transmutation (recreating the original features of the outer energies).

The transformation and transmutation work are generally done by advanced incarnating LPRF1 PES (planetary souls) since the younger souls, still in training, are mostly working with the ability to control and administer the outer form and in this learn by experience how to control and purify the emotional and mental layers connected to the outer form.[40] All LPRF1 PES incarnate using the methods of projection, projecting a chosen part of their consciousness composition into the

---

[38] The last 50.000 years – give and take - the regressed races has attempted and succeed to some degree in taking over our reality field is nothing in the big scope of things. Besides, the regressed races have only got control of a small percentage of the overall LPRF1 planetary system.

[39] As we learn in *Destiny of Souls* there are many restoring programs for the energy systems incarnating here engineered to adjust and heal them after each lifetime.

[40] This work is nicely explained in the testimonies found in Michael Newton´s books. It has to be remembered that most of the accounts found in *Journey of Souls* are from lower leveled souls, whereas much more details are given in *Destiny of Souls*; hence I recommend reading the book *Destiny of Souls* to get a clear picture of the work of the inner non-solidified root races (the "souls"). Most of the former root races are now only part of the non-solidified worlds, albeit new souls are generated all the time to follow with the development and the changes instigated by the LPRF2s, controlling the current outer areas.

outer areas where this portion merge with the brain and CNS of the human form, leaving the original non-solidified energy system behind in a less productive state, all depending on the level of maturity of the soul genetics.

The integration process of the LPRF1 PES is done voluntarily and is very dissimilar to the forced incarnations of the non-viable stellar LOES existing in the reintegration areas under the timeline collective.

The LPRF1 PES incarnates to develop the genetics, to progress and to transmute the outer areas, whereas the non-viable stellar LOES are forced into the outer areas to produce specific forms of energy to sustain their owners.[41] The re-integration areas are placed on the astral plane, whereas the non-solidified energy systems and their consciousness compositions, i.e. planetary souls or LPRF1 PES, exist in the middle and upper LPRF1 areas of the controlled four timelines as well as in all of the areas of the non-controlled other 8 timelines.

It is possible to work in the outer reality fields without a physical form as we see evidence of in direct telepathic contact from stellar as well as planetary humans in non-solidified form.

It is also possible to enter the outer areas as non-solidified energy systems directly, which I have experienced in conversations with discarnates as well as the early visits from my teacher Merak, when I began to wake up. In both cases the discarnates enter our reality field and from that medium are able to manifest to such an extent that we can see, feel and hear them.

The Destroyed LPRF1 Network
There is not much to add to this level yet, because I only have a vague understanding of the original LPRF1 network. It was created to enable the inner root races to work in the unstable LRPF1 lower areas after

---

[41] All accounted for in the book *Understanding the Old Stellar Souls*.

the timeline event. Today it is a destroyed stratum of energy.[42] It is part of the planetary morphogenetic field and the planetary gridwork and it holds the features created by the engineers to some extent.[43] It was destroyed in one of the many wars that have taken place here and I think it finally broke down during the Reptilian Riots, between the outer and inner races seeking to gain control of the LPRF1 system. With the destruction of the LPRF1 network it was possible to alter, manipulate and re-engineer the original structure and its lifeforms, and then merge it with the sections of the PMFs of the 3rd and 5th planets i.e. the Moon and Mars transferring their codes of life to our planet, enabling the stellar races to incarnate here.

The LPRF1 network is a plane that has to be crossed to be able to enter the inner realities. This level is identical with the quantum fields, which science are able to work with. It is also the same as the quantum core fields (QCFs) as perceived by the stellar consciousness type, since the LPRF1 network and the CQF represent the 6 root races and their dissimilar morphogenetic components (quantum variables) sustaining the integrated energy systems, be it planetary or stellar.

When inner lifeforms pass the LPRF1 network they are transferred via their light quotient that pulls them across the destroyed band and into the correct plane of existence from where they entered.

This is the basic understanding of quantum bridging, when it happens naturally, albeit the transfer by light quotient can also be replicated by the use of technology, transferring energy systems and their genetics to other planes of existence in the gathered LPUs.

---

[42] Often described by the inner lifeforms as a murky grayish yellow level of energy from which they transfer from the outer to the inner planes of existence (repeatedly reported by the inner lifeforms as they leave the outer areas and enter the inner in the work of Micheal Newton).

[43] Here we go into one of the many different functions of the inner realties and their lifeforms, including engineers of planets in the outer manifestation belt.

The Astral Plane

The astral plane is the result of the astral barrier, the total sum of connected chakra systems and the resulting human emotionality, the collective sum of auras and the subconscious material these holds.

The astral plane is an artificial layer of energy only visible and accessible via the human psyche because it is created by the human psyche. It is positioned between the 3rd and 4th dimensions and is an artificial interdimensional level or space.[44]

The exact details of the barrier is well hidden in the minds of the controllers and beyond my level of understanding; however I have given some details in *the Souls of Humanity* about the construction of the barrier, linking up to the ancient crystal pillars placed in the core of our reality. The astral barrier is an extension to the pillars, using the crystalline sciences to reverse the emission fields of the pillars as well as linking up the chakra system to this through the fragmented genetics in the core of the chakras.[45]

The pillars were initially put there to stabilize the gridworks of the lower LPRF1 areas due to the impairment of the LPRF3 levels in the khundarays that followed after the timeline event. Now that is all we need to know. It is easy to get lost in the details of any construction, which is a sort of mental distortion, and it is not as much how things are constructed that matters, but what we do with the understanding

---

[44] This means that it is not visible to the non-solidified energy systems and their consciousness compositions (the individual LPRF1 Planetary Energy System, i.e. the LPRF1 PES) when they leave the outer areas and return to the inner areas. In other words, they do NOT pass through the astral and mental planes when they leave. However the astral souls do pass through the astral and mental planes because they are part of these.

[45] The connection is here to be seen as entanglement more than a direct thread or remote control. The programming is inserted into the pillars through the crystalline technologies and from there the fragments in the core of the chakras respond to the "signal" that is emitted from the pillars, controlling the human mind and emotions. The genetic fragments are coded to fit specific programs inserted into specific pillars; hence each individual chakra system is connected to different pillars.

we have got. That is: we only need to know enough to work with it; not all the gory details. We have to be able to see the forest for the trees, so to speak.

The astral plane has developed ever since the astral barrier was put into play around 2500 BCE. As humanity utilized the chakra system imposed to their periphery nervous system as well as central nervous system, controlling the energies of the body, they grew accustomed to the astral energies they produced, while responding to the programs of the barrier. The human psyche, which is the same as the astral body, developed in that period and has not changed much since.[46] Consequently the astral plane is manmade for most parts, made from the thoughts and emotions of man during the last 4,500 years.

Over the period the barrier worked, when a specific program was set in motion by the astral barrier, it initiated an impulse affecting the stellar fragments in the core of the targeted chakras (in the beginning as astral energy holding stellar fragments and later on as mental energy holding galactic fragments).

From the activation of the core, energies would then be produced affecting the perimeter of the chakras, making them spin. The spin of the perimeter emits a certain type of frequency and this frequency initiates a cascade of electro-chemical reactions in the body via the glands and the periphery nervous system, when we talk about the lower chakras, whereas the throat and heart chakras are affected by

---

[46] Read the epic of Gilgamesh from Sumer dated to around 2100 BCE and you will see that the intrigues, human desires and how to respond to that have not changed much. The difference is that back then brutality was part of the daily experience made into entertainment in times of peace, such as the gladiator games in ancient Rome, and a natural part in times of war or political unrest. The same level of brutality is still present in our reality; however the entertainment of today is not based upon real killings for common man, but made virtual in forms of games and movies. Wars and the urge to kill is still a deep part of the programming of man.

the electric impulses caused by the central nervous system; i.e. more mental oriented programs.

No human on this planet is literally free in mind and emotions.

The astral plane has grown significantly over the last 2,000 years and the Middle Ages with its dark magic and religious systems made new areas of the astral plane into which all sorts of entities and astral lifeforms came to life.

Naturally the earlier blood sacrifices performed by indigenous people all over the world added the initial levels to the astral plane of astral entities with their shamanistic rituals, producing many forms of astral entities and astral lifeforms; including the level where the LPRF2 dark ones, only having an astral body as their primary form, exist and thrive on the astral energies produced by the ego-triangles of perverted men and women of all times, using the dark arts, brutality and the like to personify their innermost perverted longings and desires.

Consequently when we take up the task of reconstructing the LPRF1 PES using the cleansed chakra system, we have to learn to control the sea of astral energies we are emerged into; there is no escaping this and all illusions of getting rid of the chakra system and hence lose the connection to the astral plane is nothing but a mere illusion.

Yes, if the chakra system is removed, there will be no response to the astral plane, since the tool to perceive it is gone and thus there is no reaction in the body and psyche. That generates a sensation of peace and quietness in the mind and body; however the tool to protect, cleanse and alter the aura is gone and with this, the power to take control of the inner worlds as well. The price of peace from the astral plane by removing the chakras is far higher than the time it takes to learn to control the chakra system and from there learn how to deprogram the chakras in order to take back the control of the physical body and mind.

The chakra system is not all bad. When cleansed enough through the purification process[47] we can use the astral and mental energies to our benefit, since they are an intrinsic part of our energy system today, as well as do our part to take the artificial layers down and remove them from the planetary gridwork.

The chakra system can transfer energy both ways; into the chakras and out from the chakras.

All in all, it is our job, as the awakening humanity of this system to cleanse up the mess instigated by the LPRF2 humanoids and performed by man; nobody else will. The fear of being controlled has to be overcome by the courage to do whatever it takes, to take back the control of the chakra system, the pillars and the gridwork.

When this is said, it is also important to acknowledge that certain areas of the astral plane are never going to be cleansed out. The areas that are totally controlled by the astral plane have to go into evaporation.

This follows the information the LPRF2 humanoids have given us i.e. the decay of our reality field, acknowledging the fact that the barrier and astral plane have destroyed a lot more than what has been contributed in certain timelines; thus we are to discern which of the 4 timelines that can be cleansed, when freed from the LPRF2 stellar humanoids and what they leave behind of technologies, and which timelines with all that is connected to them, we have to let go.

The Astral Body
The astral body, generated out of energies from the astral plane, is the basis of the chakra system. The astral body is the basics of the

---

[47] The first steps of how to cleanse and learn to counteract the programs of the astral barrier is taught in the SETAH Fundamentals.

human psyche, controlling the mind and emotions of common man. *The astral body holds 7 layers to be cleansed and worked through:*

1. The merged auras of the parents lay the chakra blueprint.[48]
2. The karmic imprinter (a 5 layered device) inserted into the core of the chakra blueprint.
3. The chakra blueprint itself.
4. The instinctual layer with coding stemming from the karmic imprinter, affecting the genetic fragments in the center of the chakras.
5. The emotional layer transmitting the coding from the astral barrier, generating the perimeter of the chakras.
6. The subconscious layer with suppressed energetic interaction potential of the aura, i.e. energy patterns. What is generated into energetic patterns in the aura is controlled by the karmic device and the programming from the astral barrier. This layer determines the perception field of the ego-triangle.
7. The collective archetypical layer; i.e. the bridge into the astral plane itself.

The first six layers are connected to the individual aspect of the astral plane and contain what we have got from our parents, the karmic imprinter and the programming of the chakras.

From the fundamental layers we use what we have got to create energy patterns. The energy patterns are created by our energetic interactions, thought forms and emotional reactions.[49] The energy patterns hold our memories, fantasies and suppressed psychological content. The subconscious is thus our energy patterns and together with the other five layers, they create our aura. The content and what

---

[48] Learn more about the chakra blueprint:
http://toveje.dk/onewebmedia/Chakra%20Blueprint.pdf
[49] All of this is explained in *Terralogy*.

we meet on the astral plane is therefore individual and depends on the composition of energies and fragments in the chakra system as well as the subconscious layer; it is therefore impossible to give a satisfying overview of the different levels the astral plane actually consists of. Let's just say that for every man and woman there is an individual section of astral entities, fantasies and realities reflecting that man or woman´s conscious and subconscious content.[50]

In spite of this, a rough overview can be given:

1. Low astral level; the residual plane of the dark arts.
2. Ghost level; haunted souls that are not willing to leave.
3. Dream level; subconscious material – fantasies – dreams.
4. Collective consciousness field; archetypes – entities.
5. Astral entities and elementals (LPRF2 fragments).
6. Nature spirits and nature devas (LPRF3 fragments).
7. Mountain, lake and sea devas (LPRF3 minor clusters).
8. The four world corners; huge entities with LPRF4 traits.
9. The reincarnation areas under the LPRF2s.
10. LPRF2 network; 4th dimension (home of the LPRF2s here).

The more we work with the perimeter of our chakras, the more we work with these 10 levels.[51] In our cleansing process we encounter the energies and their corresponding content on the astral levels; all in all what matches our subconscious, which is also build up in layers of different types of astral energies, as well as the energetic content of our astral body as it unfolds in our cleansing work.

We go from the normal human emotions, to the subconscious, to the collective and so forth and in this journey we also probe deeper

---

[50] We go into and work with this content in the SETAH Therapy.
[51] All depending on what type of soul we have got.

into the astral body itself, releasing and cleansing the deepest levels of this until we finally are able to view and release the merged field of our parents auras, which brought about the foundation of our astral body. When this level is reached, we are in full control of our astral body and thus we know how to handle all forms of astral energies.

The Mental Plane
The mental plane is as such not a real plane, compared to the astral plane that contains worlds of entities living there and to an extent unfold a form of artificial evolution.

The mental plane is a new invention from around the 1700's. It is mostly composed of thought forms and is a belt of frequencies holding thoughts and ideas. Thoughts are the product, or emission field, of brain waves and the mental plane therefore corresponds to the brain wave frequencies found in human and animal brains.

Each frequency band[52] corresponds to a specific type of energy that produces specific types of thought forms in the brain that ignite the neurons and synapses in a certain way, creating brain functions and chemical reactions in the body.

The brain wave frequencies can be compared to a set of coding, holding a specific amount of mental energy which makes the electric circuits of the human and animal body on a cellular level respond to the mental plane and the LPRF3 network on different levels; all from the encoded sections of the leylines to the network implemented into the quantum fields.

The mental plane affects both the human morphogenetic field as well as the planetary morphogenetic field. These alterations are seen on quantum, atomic and molecular level, changing the core of the

---

[52] Here I talk about the brain wave frequencies, i.e. the alpha, beta, delta, theta and gamma waves.

cells and in this the basic structures of the bio-DNA.[53] Again as with the astral plane, the layers we can see reflect our composition and chakra system.

A general view of the mental plane:
1. Low mental level; bugs and residuals from the dark arts.
2. Human thought forms.
3. Lower LPRF2; working area for the LWBs.
4. Higher LPRF2; working area for those serving the LPRF3s.
5. Field of LPRF3 fragments.
6. Lesser infected LPRF3s existing as clusters in the higher frequency bands of the mental plane.
7. LPRF3 network; 5th dimension (home of the LPRF3s here).

The Mental Body
The mental body is the mind-field. It is positioned around the head but it also stretches into the rest of the body due to the connection to the cores of the chakras and the link up from them to the central nervous system. It affects all electric circuitry in the body, but it also affects the core of the cells.

The mind-field alters the DNA from inside and out, whereas the astral plane affects the cells from outside and in. The mind-field holds energetic patterns generated by the thought forms we utilize often. The more we work with a set of beliefs, the more they literally turn into rigid energy patterns, clogging our mind-field and in this forcing the brain to work within limited ranges of frequencies.

---

[53] The bio-DNA is also affected by astral energies, i.e. epigenetics.

The perimeter holds at least 10 levels that have to be worked with, all depending on the chakra blueprint:

1. Low astral level; the residual plane of the dark arts.
2. Ghost level; haunted souls that are not willing to leave.
3. Dream level; subconscious material – fantasies – dreams.
4. Collective consciousness field; archetypes – entities.
5. Astral entities and elementals (LPRF2 fragments).
6. Nature spirits and nature devas (LPRF3 fragments).
7. Mountain, lake and sea devas (LPRF3 minor clusters).
8. The four world corners; huge entities with LPRF4 traits.
9. The reincarnation areas under the LPRF2s.
10. LPRF2 network; 4th dimension (home of the LPRF2s here).

The Construction of a Chakra

Chakra Perimeter

Chakra Core

Mental Energies

Astral Energies

The core holds at least 7 levels that have to be worked with, all depending on the chakra blueprint:

1. Low mental level; bugs and residuals from the dark arts.
2. Human thought forms.
3. Lower LPRF2; working area for the LWBs.
4. Higher LPRF2; working area for those serving the LPRF3s.
5. Field of LPRF3 fragments.
6. Lesser infected LPRF3s existing as clusters in the higher frequency bands of the mental plane.
7. LPRF3 network; 5th dimension (home of the LPRF3s here).

The Progression Pyramid

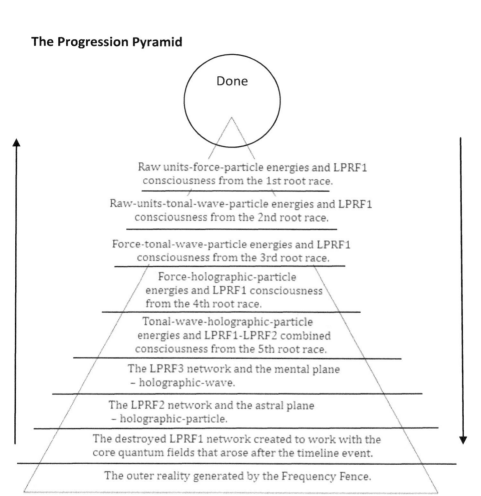

Done

Raw units-force-particle energies and LPRF1 consciousness from the 1st root race.

Raw-units-tonal-wave-particle energies and LPRF1 consciousness from the 2nd root race.

Force-tonal-wave-particle energies and LPRF1 consciousness from the 3rd root race.

Force-holographic-particle energies and LPRF1 consciousness from the 4th root race.

Tonal-wave-holographic-particle energies and LPRF1-LPRF2 combined consciousness from the 5th root race.

The LPRF3 network and the mental plane – holographic-wave.

The LPRF2 network and the astral plane – holographic-particle.

The destroyed LPRF1 network created to work with the core quantum fields that arose after the timeline event.

The outer reality generated by the Frequency Fence.

The progression pyramid is the mountain we have to climb to be able to progress out of our imprisonment and artificial modifications. We have to begin from below and work our way from the outer reality to the inner, and continue the cleansing, raising our energies in the chakras to the level, where they are not controlled by the astral, mental planes, or the remaining LPRF2 races existing here. When the planetary core is reached, we begin the reconstruction of the LPRF1 PES and the outer plane by transforming the lower planes of existence using the inner and higher planes to do so.

The Distribution of Souls

As we go deeper into the work and understanding of our reality field, the knowledge of the various types of souls present here becomes important. Again we work with the concept of an inner reality, which many perceive as the spirit worlds but as a matter of fact these areas are the main part of the realities existing in the LPUs.

The LPRF1 system with its outer manifestation field.
In the outer areas we find organic-solidified lifeforms and beyond the LPRF1 network (the quantum fields) we find inner frequency realities (planes of existence) composed of higher forms of energies producing a plethora of energy systems, i.e. non-solidified lifeforms into which the soul genetics from the first universe as well as the LPU can progress.

All souls, i.e. the non-solidified energy systems with specific genetic compositions, called composite consciousness, stem from the highest sphere of reality, i.e. the LPRF5 level in our section and its raw consciousness fields unfolded beneath all reality fields of the LPU. In the gathered LPU (the G-LPU) the LPRF5 level is found in what we call the core. The core is not really a core as we think of it, but the highest vibrating level of existence, that could be seen as the top of a cone.

The highest plane of existence is the central point of creation from where all genetics, energies and lifeforms originate.[54]

The highest plane of existence is found as the core in all systems (seen as the core, because this central level is interconnected with the LPRF5s, sustaining the entire reality field), be it LPRF3, LPRF2 or LPRF1 and the ones in between.

This level is identical with the templar, i.e. the core energy system, whether it is unfolding a galactic nebula, a stellar sun or a planet. In other words, the energy system of a reality field is the manifestation of the merged LRPF4-LPRF5 and can thus be seen as the lifeforms of the merged LRPF4-LPRF5s, although a templar at the nebulae level is more complex than the templar found in a planetary system. Hence the collected corpus of templars is the energy system of the LPRF4-LPRF5s, represented in all reality fields as the templar of that reality field producing the pulsating energy of the core in that system.

Most lesser developed souls (let's just call them souls but keep in mind that they are the non-solidified energy systems with composite consciousness and that they are a lifeform from different reality fields of the G-LPU and not spirits[55]) are incarnating in planetary systems, whereas more advanced souls use the higher reality fields in the G-

---

[54] It is only the advanced souls that have the understanding of the source of souls as being identical with a group of ancient entities, existing on a very high plane of existence aka the LPRF5s (my books as well as the *Journey of Souls*, page 189 giving the conclusions of this from an interview of case 23).

[55] The idea of spirit and souls stem from our cultural belief systems where a soul is directly spawned from the godhead or "Source". Here the idea is that all souls are a reflection of the godhead and are perfect, god-like entities going into incarnation to "save" the world or has fallen here, and other new spirituality systems. I can only recommend the *Destiny of Souls* by Michael Newton (2000), which shows a totally different picture. The word *soul* also goes back to Greek ideas, reproduced into Christian thought forms and the belief systems. Thus whenever we use the word *soul* we have to be aware of what belief system we subconsciously tap into and what type of energy we are pulling in by doing this; hence the use of the LPRF3 LTOS (galactic souls), the LPRF2 LOES (stellar souls) and LPRF1 PES (planetary souls) to denote the non-solidified lifeforms from these planes of existence.

LPU to express their genetics. Again here we have to remember that we have left our isolated scope of things, i.e. the four timelines under the timeline collective, and have entered the other 8 as well as the G-LPU where things work in a different way; i.e. there are functional LPRF3s and LPRF2s, as well as the LPRF1 planetary souls incarnating in the many versions of the G-LPU as well as the newly formed outer areas, using the energies of the timeline event to generate planets similar to the ones in our LPU.[56]

The Human and Animal Counterpart

Before we look at the souls incarnating on our planet, i.e. in the outer manifestation fields which also include the 11 other planets in our planetary system, we have to remember that the human and animal forms are designed only to this planet.

The current human form is, as we know, a genetically upgrading of the primates that were engineered and seeded into the 4th planetary system. Again here we have to grasp that the outer manifestation fields and their physical appearance were not natural to our LPU[57] to begin with. They arose after the timeline event. However as it was a fact that these forms of energy existed, new lifeforms were created out of them and became the natural manifestation energy used in the 4th planetary system, as well as in the end times of the colonies of the 3rd planetary system, into which the inner human races could explore

---

[56] Working with the outer energies and areas does not automatically imply to work on what is called enslavement planets. The enslaved planets and systems under the control of the regressed ones, including the technological new stellar races, are a subsiding era in history. It's only in our quadrant that the regressed races continue to block any forms of progress by consciousness, relying entirely on technology. Most of the systems in the G-LPU utilize a balanced use of technology and consciousness, having learned from our LPU. Regression systems, as seen in the archaic primitive controlling factions of our planetary system, are not found anywhere else in the LPU.
[57] The LPU - the less progressed universe – denotes the types of genetics dissimilar to the soul genetics found in the first universe.

the newly created outer reality fields as root races.[58] The original outer after timeline energies functioned in a very dissimilar way than the one we are accustomed to today. Present day energies on our planet are infused with astral and mental energies. For now I have little knowledge of how far the astral and mental energies stretch into the rest of the solar system, affecting the other planets.

All I know is that there are many worlds out there similar to the other 11 planets in our system, using the after timeline event type of energy to engineer planets and stellar systems, although all of these systems and planets have their original planetary morphogenetic field (the quantum core fields) intact and thus the after timeline event energies in these systems are connected to and worked with, involving direct contact of the minds of the inner races, i.e. by the use of consciousness.[59]

Primarily animals and plants were engineered[60] to unfold in the 4th planetary system, using the same type of consciousness technologies that were utilized in the Sirian Workstations. As we have learned the 4th root race were more or less these animals and plants, although they also existed as a higher form of race in the lesser dense sections of the 4th planet. We find descriptions of these higher lifeforms in the Vedas, i.e. the Asuras and the Suras. The higher forms of the 4th root race gave the blueprint to the outer human form (the homo sapiens lineage and not the other prior species that were to the core other

---

[58] The 1st and 2nd root races of the before timeline event worlds, and to some extent the 3rd, were also exploring the areas of the LPRF1 system but in a different fashion natural to the original purpose of the LPRF1 system. They too worked with the different areas of our system to develop it and in this progressing by mastering the forms of energies this system held. Today our planetary system, and others alike, holds different energies but the purpose is the same; progression of consciousness and mastery of energy.

[59] *Journey of Souls* and *Destiny of Souls* give to some degree information regarding this but it is also said that this level of information is prohibited and cannot be reveal yet.

[60] *Destiny of Souls* gives some fine accounts of how this is done by the inner races.

forms of primates such as the homo erectus), using their genetics and energetic makeup to develop and upgrade the primate genetics. The primate genetics were used because they were the highest lifeform on the 4th planet and had the correct bio-DNA from which a similar, but more advanced, lifeform could be created.

This implies that homo sapiens was a creation of the inner realities and not of the stellar races. Whenever I go into this, it is complicated to discern who created what. However I believe that the Neanderthal species were an attempt from a stellar faction of the colonies, also operating on the 4th planet, to generate their version of a planetary outer form, able to hold their genetics and inner energy systems.

I believe that they used the BEF[61], we came to know in *Terralogy*, as their blueprint. The later created homo sapiens were engineered to house the energy systems of the LPRF1 planetary souls and in this were to develop a higher form of civilization on this planet; i.e. a form of caretakers, transforming and transmuting the energies of the 4th planet.

This way of viewing the creation of the present day human form is dissimilar to the account I gave in *Terralogy*; the point is to give a fair understanding of the different human forms utilized by the different souls, there actually are present here.

The point being is that there have been both stellar and planetary engineers involved in present day human and animal forms, as well as the later mix of bio-DNA that took place around 2500 BCE.

Humans today are a mix of the original outer human races that were engineered to hold the planetary and stellar (back when they were not warring against each other) integration portion of the inner races (i.e. the soul of the outer human body) and it is complicated to distinguish genetically speaking; perhaps the only remnants of the many variations of an outer human form able to hold the souls of the

---

[61] BEF – biologically engineered forms.

inner realities, are to be traced in the different blood types.[62] The last important thing is to remember that the outer human form, including animals as we saw in *Terralogy*, have a chakra system engineered to create a psyche functioning as a faculty to sense and structure the energetic input and interpret it.

Without the psyche, aka the chakra system, the human and animal forms would not be able to exist, function and navigate on their own in this reality.[63] Of course the chakra system is also the medium into which the different souls, *i.e. the integration portion of the inner races,* integrate themselves and from this level, learn to take control over and handle the organic counterpart.

This means that the organic counterpart[64] has an ego or sense of self, whether it is in animals or humans, that is functional and do not need a soul to work.[65]

The chakra system, in humans and animals, holds stellar fragments in the core of the chakras, functioning as the operator of the chakra system. The cores are linked to the barrier and its programs. First the astral programs of the stellar LPRF2s were installed and later the mental programs were added by the galactic LPRF3s.

---

[62] Blood types could very well be the key to figure out what type of soul that is connected to the chakra system, because the soul genetics have to match the bio-DNA to be able to link up to the human form.

[63] Which naturally take us to the chakra removal thing: After some consideration and remembering some cases I had of chakras being "removed", I have come to the conclusion that they are not removed, but merely sealed in by an artificial crystalline energy field.

[64] Or host-bodies; as they are called in the *Destiny of Souls*.

[65] This is confirmed in the *Destiny of Souls* over and over again, i.e. that the portion of the inner non-solidified energy system (i.e. the inner human) merges with the outer organic form around 4-6 months into the pregnancy and that the host already has a sense of self, i.e. an ego. This ego and the portion of the inner human then have to learn to cooperate. The inner humans DO NOT integrate themselves into animal forms.

The chakra system was and is set up to produce all considered necessary thoughts and emotions to make the organic counterpart functional. In this the organic counterparts would and still do produce all needed forms of astral and mental energies, required to keep the artificial structures of our reality working. These artificial structures were implemented into the planetary morphogenetic field using the astral barrier.

All spiritual teaching systems, i.e. the teachings of how to learn to collaborate with the soul, have their foundation in:

- Learning to handle emotions (mindfulness and awareness).
- Learning to handle thought forms (meditation - inner silence).
- Learning the handle the body (control of desires and needs).
- Developing the intuition (listening to the inner voice).
- Developing the connection to the inner observer.
- Re-connecting to the soul/higher self.
- Let the soul/higher self take over.

None of this is new. What is new is what soul (planetary or stellar) or higher self (galactic, i.e. LPR3) the organic counterpart is connecting to and take instructions from, that is what agenda the human is to unfold into this world, once it has reconnected to the "walk-in", which is perhaps a more adequate term for the soul-merging humans experience today.

In the ancient days the merging was not perceived as a walk-in by the ego, because the ego of the first human forms wasn't there; the ego we know of is a product of the astral barrier and the chakra system. The chakra system was not present in the first humans, which were mere empty shells awaiting the integration of the inner resident; i.e. the operator as we learned of in *Terralogy*. Both the planetary and stellar races used the human forms to work in the environment of the 4th planet.[66] As the barrier came up, the inner planetary and non-regressed inner stellar races of the G-LPU did not stop integrating themselves into the 4th planetary system. However they did not do this as the sole operator; instead they walked-in by projecting a portion of their essence from their non-solidified energy system (i.e. the inner human holographic form) and merged this with the ego generated by the chakra system.

It should thus be clear that the outer organic forms with their chakra systems, produced after the inserted astral barrier, were not supposed to have a non-solidified co-operator from the inner realms. This came to be by agreements and deals made by the brotherhoods, under the supervision of the right wing brotherhood (the RWBs has always teamed up with the original LPRF1 root races), who argued for the beneficial results of a continuing integration into the human form, now engineered and administered by the controllers, and in this continuing the root race program instigated by the LPRF1 inner races and their engineers of the 4th planet, before the takeover.

The Animals on our Planet

Most animals on our planet are not infused with animal LPU genetics but are a mere product of the astral barrier, holding fragments similar to the ones found in human clones. Animals do have an ego, but it is a prefabricated one; the exception is animals close to humans. They are strongly affected, via horizontal merging, by the chakra system of their humans and from this display the emotional and mental state of their owner in a semi-human or animalistic form. Some animals hold minor astral entities acting as an animal soul and a few animals, if

---

[66] Again we are here talking about an era where the 4th planet thrived and unfolded lifeforms under the controlled progression and evolution by the root races of the inner realities. The root races thus exist as an inner and outer form. Today they mostly exist as the inner forms, i.e. the planetary souls integrating themselves into the host-bodies engineered by the controllers.

their owners are integrated planetary souls, hold the original animal LPRF1 consciousness which is not to be seen as souls but the original 4th planetary type of animal consciousness that unfolded in the 4th root race in the lower lifeforms.

The Distribution of Souls on our Planet
Our planet, i.e. under the timeline collective, holds around 7 billion people. Souls from different sectors are integrated into most of these 7 billion human counterparts outliving the different agendas.

The Allocation of Souls[67]
    30% Clones (ca. 2.1 billion people)
    15% Astral Souls (ca. 1.05 billion people)
    15% Dormant Stellar LOES (ca. 1.05 billion people)
    10% Activated LPRF2 Stellar LOES (ca. 0.7 billion people)
    20% Planetary not fully activated LPRF1 PES (ca. 1.4 billion people)
    10% Hybrid Souls (ca. 0.7 billion people)
    A tiny amount of Mission Souls (in the thousands, nothing more)

The Clones on our Planet
The human form can easily function without a higher principle, or soul attached to them. 30% of humans on our planet are clones. This means that they only have a chakra system preprogramming them to function in our reality as "humans".

They have feelings and thoughts but very little, that comes from them, are out of the ordinary when we talk about clones. They are not extremely bright or clever. They work, they eat and drink, they fornicate without further thought and in this they add tremendously to the overpopulation, they sleep and they produce lots and lots of

---

[67] I here use the nice round number 7 billion even though we are 7.4 billion (2016). http://www.worldometers.info/world-population/

astral and lesser forms of mental energies; exactly what they were engineered to do.

All in all the clone program is a program totally out of control[68] cf. the ongoing projects to take out the surplus of them. The clones do not respond well to the chemical additives, chemtrails etc because these projects are targeted to mess up their biological chemistry, among other things.

The Astral Souls on our Planet

The astral soul segment is a special area. They are ancient stellar souls that came here in the first days of the draco-reptilian reign. Some of them entered our system voluntarily from mostly avian systems, although most of them were brought here as prisoners of the Reptilian Riots; i.e. as slaves. They were then detached from their holographic-particle bodies and their energy systems, with the stellar genetics, were sealed off and used by the controllers in various functions in the pre-astral barrier reality.

As things changed and the astral barrier came up, the ancient stellar souls became the main carriers of the barrier program until the clones effectively were implemented into the outer areas. From then on the ancient souls, sealed off with a non-functional personality, were re-circulated and used to sustain the barrier and our reality.

Today most of these ancient souls are not recognizable from the clones except from their more advanced and distinguished mindset.

The astral souls can be revived and altered into a planetary soul however it takes the full commitment of the current organic form, collaborating with a higher positioned soul in human form to regain the viability of the stellar genetics.

---

[68] It is quite common for the different programs on this planet that they spin out of control, as with the weather modification programs. These have totally destroyed the "natural" weather patterns for this planet aka the programs that were created by the ancient root races of the colonies.

The LPRF2 Dormant Stellar LOES on our Planet

The dormant stellar LOES are part of the LWBs or the controllers in some of the after 1959 alien programs. They have been inserted to sustain and assist in the making of the new forms of human bio-DNA.

The dormant stellar LOES are all sealed off. Some of them look like non-functional LOES, i.e. astral souls. In both cases most of them are not aware of their function here. They have not chosen to incarnate; instead they have been inserted by the ones that owns these energy systems. The dormant stellar LOES are kept in a hibernated state in the 4th and 5th dimension and are only put into the outer reality to do the bidding of their owners.

The dormant LOES have also been sealed off with a non-functional personality like the astral souls. Many of the dormant LOES came here in the same period as the astral souls; however the dormant LOES have not been misused to the same degree as the non-viable LOES due to specific combinations of LPU genetics.

The LPU genetics in the dormant LOES hold different levels of infection and regression and are in dire need of restoring and regeneration. Due to these levels of regression and infection most of them have collaborated with the LWBs in various forms over various time periods, knowingly and willingly. My three books are focused the dormant stellar LOES.

Aside from the new bio-DNA programs, they have been inserted to activate the LPRF2-LPRF3 networks, i.e. bridging the 4th and 5th dimension into our reality, making it possible to ground the teachings of the regressed stellar and infected galactic races as thought forms and actively used developmental systems.

Most of the dormant LOES are not activated or awakened on a full conscious level, only enough for them to actively seek and work with the stellar and galactic teachings. They are drawn to participate in the stellar and galactic teachings as their students or as zealous followers of the activated stellar LOES, functioning as their teachers and gurus.

The Activated LPRF2 LOES on our Planet

The activated LOES typically stem from the controllers (bloodlines) and LWBs. They are aware of their origin and function on our planet from a semi-activated state to a full-blown awareness.

The lesser activated LOES within the bloodlines work as political leaders, innovators of programs leading to extraplanetary sciences, scientist on specific projects, governmental developers, directors of large companies and so forth. They all work under strict telepathic control of a higher positioned stellar human-humanoid, controlling their ideas and desires towards the segment they have been inserted to change or control.

The full-blown activated controller LOES (i.e. bloodlines) are the hidden top figures behind the secret military and scientific projects, black ops and the like. They also function as the hidden top leaders in all formations of political, monetary and scientific committees and organizations controlling our world.

The lesser activated LWBs work as teachers of spiritual systems, religious systems or within programs supporting the ideas of eternal life, re-vitalization, after-life systems etc. They work under a master, in a master-apprentice relationship, where the master telepathically controls their ideas and desires towards the segment they have been inserted to change or control.

The semi-active LWBs function as the opposition in political and scientific programs instigated by the controllers, delaying any form of higher stellar progress into our reality.

The fully activated LOES of the LWB are not visible in the outer world, but work through different types of secret societies drumming up the religious, spiritual and other forms of inner developmental programs.

The LPRF1 PES on our Planet

The planetary souls are all incarnating by their own free will to learn and progress. They come here to learn to handle the organic form and its chakra system. It's all part of a long term goals of eventually reconstructing our planetary system into the next phase.

They have incarnated since the first organic forms were created and just because there is a bump in the road, having changed the 4th planet into what it is today, it does not change the long term goals.

The Hybrids on our Planet

The hybrid souls have incarnated since the late 1600's to improve their genetic composition. The goal is to enable them to master and handle the DNA and form of the novo sapiens, i.e. the Gray-human engineered organic form.[69]

There are also other stellar races involved in this producing other hybrid human forms. Some hybrid souls prefer to stay on this planet, in spite of their original purpose, and choose to become part of the future root races that will unfold after the great transition. In these future root races there is also a place for hybrid souls and the novo sapiens, and other human-stellar compositions.

The Mission Souls on our Planet

The mission souls are a mixed group of engineered energy systems. The energy systems of the mission "souls" are artificially constructed to meet the requirements of this planet and its current type of vessels. The mission souls are copies of original planetary souls from

---

[69] The Grays have a collection of very ancient planetary soul genetics from which they extract the building blocks to produce a new form of human.

other systems, projecting their other-planetary soul genetics into the copied engineered energy systems attached to the human body. The engineered energy systems are very similar to the ones we find in the hybrid souls.

These other-planetary souls have agreed to work with the LPRF1 planetary souls to do "the trial transition period" in 2017-2025. If we succeed in raising the energies of the planetary templar, these engineered souls will stay here, integrating more of their original planetary genetics, positioned in other systems.

Humans carrying these engineered mission souls are typically in their mid-twenties and are in the process of awakening now.

The Planetary Templar

The planetary templar is the inner energy system behind the outer manifested as well as the blueprint for the inner reality fields. The function of the templar is the same as a LOES or the LPRF1 PES behind stellar and planetary organic bodies.

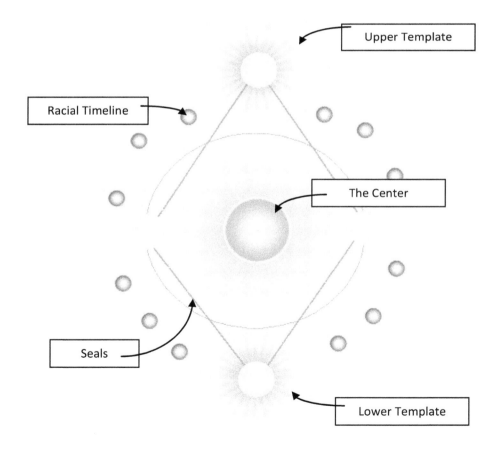

The templar is the highest plane of consciousness and energy in large manifestation fields. In our planetary templar the consciousness is built up of the fields of raw LPRF5 units merged with LPRF4 energies added with the LPRF1 features in the gridwork. It is the extension of the core in all systems because this central level is interconnected with the LPRF5s, sustaining all reality fields and their lifeforms. This goes for all templars be it the ones in the LPRF3, LPRF2 or LPRF1 systems and the ones in between. Thus a templar is the core energy system, whether it is unfolding a galactic nebula, stellar sun or planet, although a templar at the nebulae level is more complex than the templar found in a planetary system.

The templars are the manifestation of the LPRF5s in their unified field version and are to be seen as the lifeforms of the merged LRPF4-LPRF5s. Hence the collected corpus of templars is the energy system of the LPRF4-LPRF5s, represented in all reality fields as the templar of that reality field, producing the pulsating consciousness-energy into the core of that system and from there into the gridwork.

The 12 Racial Timelines
Each of the racial timelines, growing out of the planetary gridwork, has its own version and ratio of the crystal pillars emitting the needed level of field consciousness units to unfold the racial features of the root race developing their specific timeline.

The crystal pillars of the non-controlled 8 timelines in our templar are not in a state of decay. When the great transition is over, the pillars in the 4 racial timelines under the timeline collective will have been replaced and in this bring new field consciousness units into the planetary systems of the 3rd, 4th, 5th and 6th root races.

Thus each racial timeline unfolds its own version of the crystal pillars and later on, as the root races develop their consciousness units and energy, the racial timelines will have recorded all of the accumulated memories as well as the consciousness and energetic features of what that root race has unfolded on their timeline. As the root races move into other planetary systems, the racial timelines will connect to the previous timeline, adding the racial memories of the previous root race into the present racial timeline.

This means that all what the root races have developed in the collected emission field[70] of their planetary system will be transferred into the next field consciousness units of the upcoming root races and their emission fields. In the end all 12 crystal pillars will hold the same collection of racial memories and the last root race will then hold and be able to unfold all the memories, knowledge and consciousness of all of the root races that had gone before the last one.

The Upper Planetary Template
The upper template of the templar consists of the yet to be integrated raw consciousness units of the LPRF5s. These will be pulled into the center of the templar as the energies in the lower template are utilized, transforms and transmuted.

The Center
The center of the templar is the same as the core of a system. Here the raw consciousness units from the upper template and the energies of the lower template merge. The core and the racial timelines, including the gridwork that unfolds from these, are the radiation point from which all lifeforms are sustained.

As the lifeforms utilize and develop the merged consciousness-energy units, the whole templar develops along with them.

---

[70] An emission field is the end result of the transformation work with the energetic units and the consciousness of a root race constituting the different levels of the LPRF1 planetary gridwork and manifested realities.

72

The Lower Planetary Template

The lower template holds the energy units of the LPRF4s. The energy units are pulled in as the gridworks develop and utilize the energies of the 4th evolutionary system transforming these into 5th evolutionary system type of merged consciousness-energy units. Thus the lower template sustains the inner and outer manifestation fields with the needed energy units to form the inner and outer worlds.

The Seals

The seals are only placed in our segment of the templar, i.e. the four racial timelines under the timeline collective. The seals are the barrier and the key to break the seals is to break down the extensive use of astral and mental energies. Thus teaching humanity how to transform these energies, and make them do it, is the most important aspect in breaking the seals.

The Energies of the Manifestation Field

The LPRF1 gridwork consists of different areas; the core, the upper, the middle and lower areas.

The core consists of
  a. Raw units-force-particle energies (LPRF5-LPRF4-LPRF1) added with LPRF1 consciousness units from the 1st root race. Crystal pillars – temple complex.

The upper LPRF1 areas are divided into two planes and consist of
  a. Raw-units-tonal-wave-particle energies (LPRF5-LPRF3-LPRF1) added with LPRF1 consciousness from the 2nd root race.
  b. Force-tonal-wave-particle energies (LPRF4-LPRF3-LPRF1) added with LPRF1 consciousness from the 3rd root race.

The middle LPRF1 areas are divided into two planes and consist of
a. Force-holographic-particle energies (LPRF4-LPRF2-LPRF1) added with LPRF1 consciousness from the 4th root race.
b. Tonal-wave-holographic-particle energies (LPRF3-LPRF2-LPRF1) added with LPRF1 -LPRF2 combined consciousness from the 5th root race.

The two artificial planes as a result of the barrier. They consist of
a. The LPRF3 network and the mental plane – holographic-wave.
b. The LPRF2 network and the astral plane – holographic-particle.

The lower LPRF1 areas are divided into two planes and consist of
a. The destroyed LPRF1 network seen from a planetary level, or the core quantum fields seen from a stellar level.
b. The outer reality generated by the Frequency Fence.

The 12 Planets

The LPRF1 planetary system consists of 12 planets engineered to house the 12 root races. All of the physical planets in our system have an outer manifested level as well as corresponding inner areas, where the non-solidified root races exist. The 12 planets hold their own planetary morphogenetic fields and a mini templar. Thus the corpus of the merged LPRF5-LPRF4s in our system consists of one large templar and 12 mini templars united into one large field. The 12 mini templars have their own racial timelines and the root races of the other planets can choose to shift to one of the other planets to develop their consciousness units in these planetary systems.

The non-solidified root races of the 12 mini templars do not have to incarnate in the human organic form; they can choose to incarnate as gaseous beings, or clusters of dense matter, or clusters of air etc.

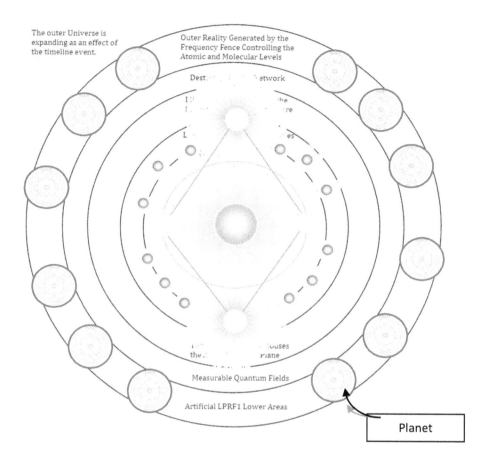

The outer Universe is
expanding as an effect of
the timeline event.

Outer Reality Generated by the
Frequency Fence Controlling the
Atomic and Molecular Levels

Dest. etwork

Measurable Quantum Fields

Artificial LPRF1 Lower Areas

Planet

There are no limitations to what outer form the inner races can take, if they wish to work and progress on one of the outer 12 planets. The environment on the 12 planets poses a chance to develop control of the outer energies as they have unfolded on the 12 planets. There are thus 144 different schools[71] in our planetary system, where the inner

[71] All in all there are 12 times 12 root races since each planetary system has 12 racial timelines and there are 12 planets. This amounts to the magical number 144. The 144 schools are centered on the process of learning to create in the outer energies and how to transform them. Transmutation is only for the advanced classes.

root races of the 12 planetary systems learn how to exist in the outer areas. The 144 schools are reflected in the areas of the inner reality fields where different planetary souls exist when they are out of incarnation. On one level the different planets represent one root race, i.e. the 3rd planetary system represents the 3rd root race and yet our planet, the 4th planetary system, has its own 12 racial timelines and in this its own version of the 3rd root race incorporated into the crystal pillars in the core of our planet. We can call these the sub-root races. This can be confusing but it is just one of the higher levels of awareness we have to deal with as something our logical mind cannot fully comprehend. To make it simple we thus refer to each of the 12 planets as holding one main root race, as I have taught up until now.

The 12 planets are[72]

1. Unknown name
   (a planet hidden behind the sun)
2. Mercury
3. Venus
4. Moon
5. Earth
6. Mars
7. Jupiter
8. Saturn
9. Neptune
10. Uranus
11. Unknown name
12. Unknown name

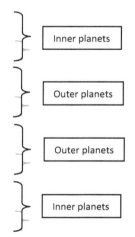

Inner planets

Outer planets

Outer planets

Inner planets

---

[72] The listing of the planets shown here are pre-timeline event numerations. After the timeline event, the outer 3rd root race was positioned on the Moon and the inner levels of them still existed on Venus, which in that version is non-solidified. The outer planet Venus arose when the sun was put into place, changing the planets in our system and their positions. Inner planets mean that the ratio of energy-consciousness leans towards the consciousness side. Outer means that the ratio leans towards the energy side.

The Sun

The Sun is foreign to our planetary system. Planetary systems are not fueled by light but by their core and gridworks. There are always stars in a planetary system but they function as gateways to the stellar realms and not as providers of energy to the forms. The energy to sustain planetary life comes from the planetary morphogenetic field.

Reconstruction work of the Planetary Templar

Recalibration technologies are connected to the crystal pillars in the other racial timelines under the governance of the Planetary Councils. The goal is to reconstruct the original planetary core and templar. These technologies will be applied to the timelines under the timeline collective as humanity progress and develops the needed energies to hold and be sustained by the higher frequencies of the original racial timelines. This will lead to the great transition.[73]

The reconstruction of the planetary templar in the section that is linked up to our timelines has to be done by humanity. Humanity is the key to breaking the seals put upon this sector.[74]

The templar seals are linked to the astral barrier; one could say that the astral barrier is the seals and that the interaction between humans on this planet and the seals has generated the astral and mental planes, restricting the planetary templar to only unfold a specific range of energies.

---

[73] The great transition will be completed in 2065 but it begins with humanity now and today. We are to do the work that will transform the bio-DNA to be able to hold and be sustained by the original planetary energies. We thus have to begin this work now. Only if we are in control of the bio-DNA are we able to do the great transition that begins in 2017. After 2025 the reconstruction technologies will amp up the gridworks in the timelines we are part of and if we are not in control of our chakra system and the bio-DNA, we will not be able to follow the lifting of energies.

[74] If humanity cannot break the seals (or the astral and mental planes) all 4 timelines go into evaporation and with them all lifeforms existing there. Then the timelines will be reconstructed from the inner root races rebuilding them.

Hence to be able to reconstruct the planetary templar, humanity has to cleanse their part of the astral and mental planes to break the spell of the astral barrier in spite the fact that it is breaking down due to the dismantling of the crystal pillars in our section. Only humanity can do this and no technology in all of the universes can undo what we have created.

We might have participated in the destruction of our own templar unwillingly and unconsciously but as we wake up and begin the transition work in ourselves, we also realize that in spite of what has been done and unfolded here, it is our planet and we are intrinsically linked to the planetary templar because it is part of the LPRF1 PES carrying the memories and knowledge of the root races that went before us. At the end of the day it is the current humanity that has to do the reconstruction work, if we want to call this our planet and if we want to be part of the LPRF1 planetary system after the great transition in 2065.

How to reach the standards outlined by the gathered LPUs

1) The astral and mental artificial planes of existence and their affect on the chakra system have to be removed and reset to their original LPRF1 lower to middle type of energy-consciousness units. Use the chakra system to reach the astral and mental planes and from this level of energetic similarity, cleanse the individual and collective fields.

- The astral components have to be cleansed and transformed into force-holographic-particle energies and re-attached to the LPRF1 consciousness type unfolded by the 4th root races. All attachments to the LPRF2 network have to be dissolved or transformed into middle LPRF1 energies.

- The mental components are to be cleansed and transformed into tonal-wave-holographic-particle energies and then re-attached to the LPRF1 consciousness unfolded by the 5th root races. All attachments to the LPRF3 network have to be dissolved or transformed into the middle LPRF1 energies.

2) The chakra system has to be freed of the main control of the ego-triangle. It is also important to lay the solar plexus and hara chakras dormant (in the purification process) or transmute them (in the advanced process).

- In this work the operator of the organic form, i.e. the ego, has to be taken into consideration as in how the ego and the stellar or planetary soul are to merge into one functioning unit.
- New levels of communication and integration procedures are to be invented. It is not possible to take control of the organic form without the full cooperation of the ego because the cellular construction is intrinsically linked to the ego and its use of the astral and mental energies.
- Transformation and transmutation work of the chakra system and with this the bio-DNA is to be done by the more advanced souls, whereas the lesser developed souls continue with the purification process, in which the ego typically is denied of its needs.
- The purification process only affects the bio-DNA in terms of purifying the perimeter and core of the cells. This is the preparation level for the transmutation work. Only the transmuted cells can follow the lift of the planetary energies.

3) The chakra system is the foundation of the rebuilding process of the LPRF1 planetary energy system (the LPRF1 PES).

The LPRF1 PES can be reconstructed from the purified chakras; i.e. the root, heart, throat, alta major, ajna and crown centre, since the blueprint of the chakra system is based upon the original LPRF1 PES.

4) From the re-constructed LPRF1 PES, the influences from the false light field on the mind-field and the affects of the astral plane on the aura have to be removed, recreating the access to the lower to the middle LPRF1 areas.

5) The present organic form has to adapt to the reconstructed LPRF1 PES. Reform the organic form to be able to hold the LPRF1 energies by transmuting the cells and bio-DNA.

6) The reconstructed LPRF1 PES has to reconnect to the planetary templar and at least 2 racial timelines aside from the present 4, with the goal of rebuilding the original manifestation fields of the 4 racial timelines under the timeline collective.

7) All organic forms choosing to do the reconstruction work are to work together and accept supervision from members of the Planetary Councils and their departments.

8) Stellar humanoids, as well as present day humans with an attached LOES, can develop their energy system into a LPRF1 PES.

9) Stellar humanoids, galactic entities and present day humans that accept and choose to make the LPRF1 system their future system, will be reborn into a LPRF1 planetary organic human form after the final

resetting in 2065, where this planetary system is reinstated into the gathered LPUs.

10) Our goal as planetary humans is first and foremost to align and incorporate the LPRF1 perception field by expanding the chiasm to cover the LPRF1 communities and at least 2 timelines aside from the ones we utilize now.

The LPRF1 Planetary Energy System

The LPRF1 Planetary Energy System

The LPRF1 planetary energy system (the LPRF1 PES) is composed of a number of centres, called this to deviate them from the vortexes of the LOES and the chakras of the organic energy system.

The Energies of the LPRF1 PES

The LPRF1 PES reflects the root races that have been developed. We have to learn to handle the energies the centres are composed of.

The root centre consists of
Raw consciousness-units-force-particle energies. It is transformed by developed LPRF5-LPRF4-LPRF1 intelligence and consciousness mix from the 1st root race.

The heart centre consists of
Raw-units-tonal-wave-particle energies. It is transformed by developed LPRF5-LPRF3-LPRF1 consciousness from the 2nd root race.

The alta major centre consists of
Force-tonal-wave-particle energies. It is transformed by developed LPRF4-LPRF3-LPRF1 consciousness from the 3rd root race.

The throat centre consists of
Force-holographic-particle energies: It is transformed by developed LPRF4-LPRF2-LPRF1 consciousness from the 4th root race.

The ajna centre consists of
Tonal-wave-holographic-particle energies. It is transformed by developed LPRF3-LPRF2-LPRF1 consciousness from the 5th root race.

The top centre consists of
All of the other possible 7 root races and their different forms of energies and consciousness.

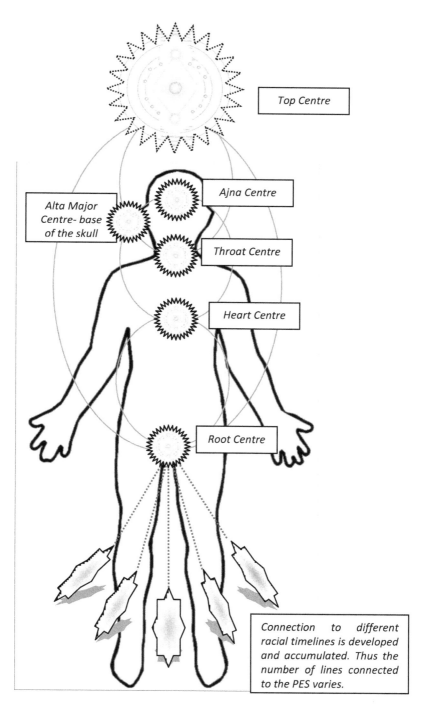

Top Centre

Ajna Centre

Alta Major Centre- base of the skull

Throat Centre

Heart Centre

Root Centre

Connection to different racial timelines is developed and accumulated. Thus the number of lines connected to the PES varies.

Reconstructing the LPRF1 PES

In the reconstruction work we are to reconstruct the chakra system, which means we have to return it to its original set up as the LPRF1 PES.

The current chakra system is an overlay system responding to the reversed technologies of the barrier and the inserted fragments in the core of the chakras, distorting the original function. In other words; the chakra system is the LPRF1 PES but it has been modified and reverse engineered to link up to the astral barrier (no the astral and mental planes) instead of the crystal pillars and the racial memory fields of the root races.

The solar plexus and the hara chakras are not natural to the LPRF1 PES either. They have to be put into a dormant state, in the purification process, freed from the barrier and other technologies that might be attached there.

In the case of rebuilding the LOES the chakra system turns into the hara quadrant and here it functions as the bridge to the stellar LOES producing the needed quanta to link these two very different systems together; however since we are not aiming for the stellar LOES, we can through the cleansing and transformation process, reconstruct the original LPRF1 PES from the chakra system. The hara quadrant is not needed in this work since we do not use the hara at all in the LPRF1 PES.

It should be noted that the energy work below is a simplification of the individual process that will unfold from within and under the instructions from the LPRF1 PES. When the chakra system is cleansed enough the LPRF1 PES, if you have done the preliminaries shown here, will begin the rebuilding process in full, releasing the steps on how to do this.

Thus this energy work is a rough guideline and cannot be done without the deeper instructions from the LPRF1 PES itself.

The Advanced Steps (only possible after 2025)

1. Refill the cleansed chakras (now called centres) with energies from the racial timelines and in this get access to the crystal pillars attached to these. This level of the crystal pillars is linked to the deepest section of the pillars, circumventing the later levels under the control of the astral barrier.

2. Use the chiasm to reconnect to the racial timelines via the centres. Remodel the core of the centres to reconnect to the planetary morphogenetic field and then to the templar core energies. The perimeter is to link up to the racial timelines. Each centre is to be reconstructed in the likeness of the planetary morphogenetic field and templar.

3. Then lay the foundation of the 1st root race into the core of the 5 centres and the top centre using the energies of the crystal pillars.

4. Then add the 2nd, 3rd, 4th and 5th root races to the core of the centres to correspond to the evolving root races. The top centre holds the potentials for the other root races, beginning with the 6th.

The chakra system has now turned into a representation of the racial timelines and is able to unfold the memories from there into the centres of the LPRF1 PES.

Use the different energies of the LPRF1 PES to activate the chiasm and reconnect to the crystal pillars and from there recreate the full LPRF1 PES, which will unfold individually all depending on the type of LPRF1 PES the reconstruction has turned it into.

A Look into the after 2025 Future

The Commodity-Exchange Economy

One way to change our present reality settings is to look at the monetary systems. A way to change things could be to turn it into a commodity-exchange economy.[75]

The commodity-exchange economy (the CEE) is a financial system used as a conversion system, because the moment we, as a species[76] in this reality field, reconnect to our soul consciousness, we will learn to handle the energetic properties of the outer rim and by this create sustainable societies that are not based upon exchange of goods for money.

The Required Settings

The commodity-exchange economy is based upon the essential assumption that we will be untied from the timeline collective, reclaiming this reality system as ours in the period after 2025, when they have to have completed their ongoing projects. "Ours" mean as a joint human race including all, i.e. the stellar and galactic races and their human forms that will choose to stay after 2025. This also includes the souls that have been dumped here for rehabilitation, the ones that have been brought here as prisoners of war, the ones that got here in the ancient restoration programs attempting to

---

[75] Another simple solution is that the ones that have loads of money share this equally with the ones that have less. But since this would only hold for a short period, we have to find sustainable solutions for the remaining period of the old settings. Naturally the great transition around 2065 has a lot to do with the new settings or outer reality and what we are aiming at.

[76] Here I am talking about the ones that choose to stay and rebuild the outer reality as part of the dismantling system.

regenerate their genetics, as well as the colonizers of the original programs and the ones that will shift side from the timeline collective as we get closer to the deadline of 2025. *All has to be forgotten and forgiven.* If we act as *one* race[77], we will proceed as one race lifting this reality field into a unity of mind, consciousness and energy.[78] All in all humans are to become a race of physical forms with integrated and active souls, positioned in the outer rim.

Naturally this economy is built upon trust and humans not being controlled by greed and mind-controlled barrier programming. Nor is it built upon a mind-set reflecting malfunctioning TEGs or infected genetics which will become more affective on the human form as the transition proceeds after 2025, elevating all levels of the outer rim and in that process pull the ones with a non-activated chakra system even deeper into the lower levels of the astral plane.[79]

Prizing in the CEE

The commodity-exchange economy is simple in its concept. Let me give an example:

If I have sown a dress, I could go to the nearest store - where I have made prior arrangements with the owner - and here present the dress to the owner of the shop. He or she would look at it and by the liking of the dress, set its value in terms of goods. Since the owner is not controlled by astral and mental implants, negative technology, or barrier programming the setting of the price would be fair and reasonable. S/he would value the dress according to the

---

[77] *One race* do not mean that we cannot hold different souls, but it entails that we acknowledge the fact that we have chosen to stay in this reality field and that we have chosen to have this type of body as our integration form.

[78] Mind is the expression of the human brain. Consciousness is mind infused with soul genetics and energy is the probability fields creating the foundation of all progression fields.

[79] The effects of this are described in both *Souls of Humanity* and *Terralogy*.

time used, the love for details and the craftsmanship that has created the dress. The material used as well as how difficult it was to get these, will be part of the prizing and the valuation of the dress. But if a piece of clothing, or any form of craftsmanship, utilizes more than one type of material and in this have to come up with different forms of materials to produce the item, such an item would be too expensive. Thus in the CEE such a commodity would not be sustainable and humanity will therefore proceed into a simpler world, where the demand for complex and time consuming goods will die out.

The Flow of the CEE

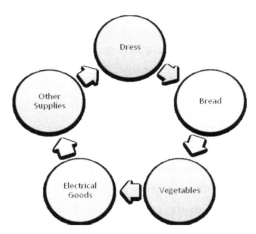

New technologies and societal structures will unfold as the soul infused geniuses amongst our race utilize their knowledge making use of the original holographic building and societal structures of the benevolent races. And in this new methods will come up to solve some of the issues we will face in the transition period.

We also have to remember that soul infused consciousness does not hold the same category of information. Planetary or stellar soul genetics give the LPRF1 planetary energy system different traits and abilities as well as what knowledge the soul has specialized in during its many incarnations in the outer rim or the systems it has traversed.

Educational Systems

In the transition period (2025-2065) old schooling systems will break down as well. The children, now free of mind-control, programming and indoctrination, will naturally unfold their inborn genetics whether they are planetary souls from other planetary systems in the gathered LPUs, having come here to do the transition with us, or they are souls awakening from the LPU races that came here during the era under the control of the timeline collective.

The children of the transition period will need guidance more than education because, as mentioned in the previous chapter, a soul is fully skilled and educated in its preferred area of expertise:

Soul infused consciousness does not hold the same categories of information. The planetary or stellar soul genetics give the LPRF1 planetary energy system different traits and abilities as well as what knowledge the soul has specialized in during its many incarnations in the outer rim or the systems it has traversed.

These children will remember their soul expertise and look for places to unfold and nurture this inborn information. The schools of the future will therefore be "hatching" institutions where the children are supervised into how to use this knowledge according to our type of reality field. Their knowledge will be focused on how to work with the holographic settings of our reality field, its artificial atmosphere and environment created by the outer rim type of energy, i.e. what we understand as electromagnetic energies. They will also look for challenges that will generate new human paradigms, i.e. societal structures, community structures etc that are based upon humans with integrated souls. All in all begin the reconstruction of the outer rim to match the worlds of other planetary systems in the gathered LPUs. Other planetary systems of the gathered LPUs are based upon holographic fluctuation fields making the holograms able to interlink directly to consciousness and in the transition period, where we alter the electromagnetic energies into holographic fluctuation fields, we are going to be the most visited system in all of benevolent areas.

Thus a higher rate of planetary souls from the gathered LPUs will incarnate here after 2025 to assist us in the transition. These souls and their human forms will also be the ones that are going to transfer the human form from the present timeline collective version into the post-transition form, which will arise after 2065. However some are to do the bridging of the old form, transforming it before the final stages of the transition and do the transition in form, altering the bio-DNA to be able to hold the new types of outer rim energies and molecules. Most of the ones doing the soul integration 2017-2065 will go out of form and then re-enter in the post-transition form.

Consequently the post-2025 children *will* need instructions in how to handle the present type of body, how to learn to control and evolve it – which will also be a part of being a parent – and the schooling systems should therefore change into a broader focus on how to behave in our society, how to contribute to the changes of the oddities, we call science and so forth.

The post-2025 children will look upon our antiquated technologies and give us ideas to unfold new ones, interconnected directly to consciousness. The educational systems have to accommodate the new ideas, assisting the incomings souls with what they need to unfold this new type of information into our society in a pace that fits the slow transformation of both the human bio-DNA and the reality field in the period 2017-2065.

We have much to learn and since the human race, those of us that stay here, is evolving into the 6th root race at some point, we bear the responsibility of connecting the past with the future and from here evolve our race into a new type of human lineage, that grew out of the timeline collective and then changed into this beautiful mix of humanoid and human genetics all infused with LPRF1 consciousness. In the future our race will bridge between the other humanoids and the human lineages from the gathered LPUs and perhaps some of the other stellar and planetary systems that have been freed of the old reign of control. We will teach these races how to reconcile and find peace in being infused on different levels.

Higher educational systems will be a further development of what was taught in primary school. Actually only 12-15 years of schooling will be required in creating a full blown educated soul infused human fit to go into our world and work here.

The goal of the educational systems is to create accepting and understanding soul infused humans, holding the required knowledge to rebuild our planetary system and in this reconnecting it to the gathered LPUs and the inner worlds.

Political and Societal Structures

The political and societal structures will break down eventually.[80]

The idea of "people elected" leaders stem from the Roman-Greek societies that unfolded as an old world order system. Hence the election of leaders will not feel natural to the post-2025 transitioning humanity.[81] We will learn from the past and know that an assembly of elders has to be built upon other criteria than the greed for power, money and personal status. The ancient Roman-Greek system of the ones in power being the nobility as well, cf. the visible factions of the

---

[80] Whether it is going to be the scenario predicted by the NOAH/NSEH as in chaotic times where a military government will take over or any other form that will arise due to the changes in our reality field.

[81] The clones will do whatever they can to keep status quo due to their programming.

controllers enjoying the game of power and greed[82], will fall and new more considerate systems will unfold.

Political Structures in Planetary Communities

The gathered LPUs planetary communities do not have hierarchical political structures; they are based upon a small group of elders carrying the knowledge of Progenitors and the progression cycles.

The elders function as supervisors because the inclusion of the knowledge from the Progenitors into the elder energy system, through the full activation of the soul genetics, provides the elders with a direct link to the purpose ad possibilities of that reality field, and in this the knowledge of what progression paths the citizens are to take and what ways that are best to build the reality field.

Crystal spheres – an outer holographic structure of the knowledge of the elders - are placed in the center of each community and all citizens can link up to this consciously, pulling in the knowledge they need to unfold their daily development of their souls, or they can address the elders directly.

In the planetary communities higher forms of experiences with the soul genetic infusion process are shared with the elders and from this integrated into the spheres. The goal of the spheres is progress and evolution, developing the members of the community. Thus lower leveled experiences will be handled within the families.

Since all soul infused races are controlled by their inner knowledge and the level of progression they have reached, there is no need for outer rules, laws and systems to direct the behavior of the citizens. All know what is best for the community and if in doubt, either the crystal spheres or the council of elders will provide solutions that can be worked with, and chosen.

---

[82] These will be less active after 2025 since the prominent ones have left and the ones that remain will have done this by free will and thus collaborate with us.

True Democracy

The democracy of the community is unfolded in town meetings where all citizens interested show up and vote regarding new things, such as letting in new incarnating souls. There are no disputes.

A democratic voting could be about what to teach a new incoming soul and what family that is the best fit. These matters would be based upon the need of the community, the soul in question and the progression rate.

The choice to procreate in planetary systems, where some sort of holographic form is utilized, is voluntarily and all depending on the societal structure, this is done by the means of natural procreation or holographic technology. Whether one or the other method is chosen, the new member of the community needs a parent or guide into how to function inside this type of world.

In the free communities we have platforms where Spheres holding
the Living Ancient Wisdom are free for all to connect to.
The Spheres are living energy since they are connected directly to
the core domains and the Ancient Ones.

We gather around, some standing others sitting in silent
meditation, and listen to the knowledge being handed to us via
the CD center in the head. The platform is placed out in the open
and all free communities I have visited have a high degree of
nature and simple living.

CD Center: the main center of
the planetary energy system.

Families in other Planetary Systems

A family is not based upon love and emotional bonding as we know of it in our world. This structure is a result of the astral programming and sexual craving systems that have been controlling humanity for eons, all instigated for procreation purposes.

The family structure in planetary systems is based upon a group of soul infused holographic forms (be it in a human form or otherwise) caring for each other because of similarities in soul genetics. Hence a family is a result of soul genetic recognition, creating what we could call a soul group.[83] These soul groups progress together and assist each other to reach the highest possible progression rate in that reality field.

The soul group is a collaboration freely instigated to assist other members in how to develop the soul genetics to the optimal settings in the holographic form, allowing them to hold more consciousness as well as how to unfold the genetics into higher levels of consciousness.

The family members support all members in this striving and the groups are often a lifelong collaboration where ups and downs in the progress are shared and valued as important information to the rest of the family.

The optimal societal structures are built upon small communities where all know each other. They are based upon families unfolding their soul group similarities, not as in opposing groups, but as a representation of the soul group progression rate evolving different aspects of the reality field, its purpose set from the Progenitors.

Our Reality Field

Since our world will turn into a conglomerate of many soul races, the post-2025 human race will adjust to this. Humanity in the future will

---

[83] Not to be confused with the new age concept of soul groups with its romantic and astral implications.

find their genetic groups or family that fits the differences in genetic makeup the best way possible. Many adjustments are to be made to make this work, but we will assist each other according to the vision we all hold of what the 4th, 5th and 6th root race are about in our planetary system[84] as well as what type of world we want to unfold to make our soul genetics unfold through the most optimal holographic settings, reaching the highest level of soul infusion.

Because the planetary souls from the other planetary systems of the gathered LPUs are incarnating in the post-2025 children (not to be confused with new souls, since most of the other planetary souls are skilled and advanced souls), their memories and knowledge of their home systems will become part of our world systems, affecting these into solutions that bridges between the current system and the one from the gathered LPUs, creating a hybrid form that suits our system in the transition period.

After 2065 nothing will resemble our present world.

---

[84] All this is explained in the TTA Self-Study 1.

About the SETAH School

The SETAH School is for all interested in learning how to do soul integration and progression. The teachings are not oriented towards specific agendas or current schools but are aimed at giving the full free choice of what agenda, teaching system and progression journey you resonate with. The courses and tools provide the needed energy work to be able to attach, integrate and activate whatever soul you have.

The SETAH Fundamentals

In the SETAH Fundamentals we begin the work with the chakra system. The chakra system is the main system controlling our emotions and thought forms. Since we are, from birth, connected to certain exterior control mechanisms such as the astral barrier in spite of its decay, the astral plane via the astral body and the mental plane via the mind-field, we have to learn how to detach the chakra system to such a degree that we regain control of our emotions, thought forms and ways of living.

Our planet is in a process of being freed from the captivators having been in full control the last 50.000 years; however only if at least 30% of humanity succeeds in activating, are we able to do the great transition 2025-2065.

The SETAH Fundamentals begin this work and from the basics, you can go into the SETAH Advanced learning to work with the stellar soul or go to the Terra Transigo Academy, where the work is focused on how to reconstruct and activate the planetary soul.

The SETAH Advanced

In the SETAH Advanced we work with the stellar soul, also called the LPRF2 LOES. In this we understand that the stellar races, called LPRF2 humanoids, have an energy system with what is called soul genetics. It is the soul genetics that link the LOES to the Progenitors, i.e. the creators of our less progressive universe (the LPU).

The Progenitors came from the first universe where the soul genetics were attached to the Source Cycles developing energy and consciousness. In this Source Cycle the work is to transform energy by the use of consciousness. This did not go entirely after the plan, which you can learn more about in my first three books as well as in the free lectures on YouTube, and this led to the LPU and the stellar humanoids, along with the other two racial types of entities in our LPU; the galactic LPRF3 and the planetary LPRF1s. Begin with the oldest videos and work your way from there.

The Terra Transigo Academy

In the Terra Transigo Academy we work with the LPRF1 planetary soul and how to reconstruct it. As it turns out the LPRF1 energy system is the foundation of the chakra system, having been reverse engineered into the chakra system. Thus it is important not to get rid of the chakra system but instead learning how to control it, administer the energies used and what type of energy we want to unfold via the chakras to our continued progression. The chakra system creates the ego and only if the ego and the integrated portion of the inner human essence are collaborating, can we reconstruct the LPRF1 energy system and from there develop new ways of what it means to be human and how to do the transition.

You find the SETAH School on www.toveje.dk

Appendix

Getting the Remaining Pieces of the Puzzle

We exist on one of the few remaining planets manifesting lifeforms in the atrophied and solidified forms of matter, which arose after the timeline event. Most of the other planets that arose back then are now long gone and their inhabitants have moved on, reconstructing the original, or similar to that, organic holographic forms of the stellar races.

Nonetheless our planet has been kept in a succession of synthetic realities into which the level one energy system and its consciousness genetics (the LOES) have been kept circulating over and over again into antiquated and unnatural lifeforms, ranging from the plant life to all the other lifeforms that inhabit our planet.

It kind of all began with a story untold in my other material. You see, the timeline event was not an accident per se but more a sort of orchestrated one, or perhaps we could say a wanted outcome of a series of experiments that unfolded in the Sirian Workstations by a group of reptoid-humans that for some or several reasons felt better than the other participants of the workstations. They had joined the groups of humanoids and human-humanoids that left the first universe and chosen to be part of the workstations to do scientific work.

The 5th evolutionary cycle of the first universe exhibited two forms of races; that is the humanoids of the 4th evolutionary cycle that had moved into the 5th and the humans.

The humans were a new type of consciousness that had arisen out of the hard evolutionary work done by the humanoids. As such they were the first of a kind and at the same time they were the summit of the humanoid races. All in all a combination of being totally new and yet the highest form of consciousness of the 5th evolutionary cycle.

Having the highest form of consciousness does not indicate being more developed but simply the peak of the consciousness traits and the possibilities they held, leading the fifth evolutionary cycle into a whole new type of reality where new consciousness traits could unfold.

It has to be understood that a peak is the pinnacle of something old and at the same time is the basic level of something new; in this the humans were both the prime races and yet they were like children in a new set of reality created from the transformation of the old worlds of the 4th evolutionary cycle, which still existed since the cycles overlaps.

The highest developed humanoids merged their developed levels of genetics (the insectoid, avian and reptoid) with mammal genetics and entered the 5th evolutionary cycle, exhibiting their highest form of consciousness, merging all of the other forms of genetics with the all-for-the-common-good mind-set of the mammals.

The mammal-humanoids became the teachers and elders of the humans and the in progress-humanoids, ensuring the progression of the fifth evolutionary humans according to the highest principles and at the same time leading the humanoids of the 4th evolutionary cycle safely into the 5th evolutionary cycle.

As a consequence the 5th evolutionary cycle elder races were for the most part humanoids and only few of the humans got a seat in the councils directing the evolutions of the lower positioned races of the first universe. This naturally created tension between the new kids on the block and the old humanoid races.

What I'm saying here is that the first universe was far from perfect and it held a lot of tensions between the humans and the humanoids, feeling superior to the humans since the humans were the new kids on the block and the humanoids the oldest races and yet the humans exceeded their consciousness traits in so many ways, which for most of the humanoids felt very unsettling and unnerving.

To come around some of these issues genetics of the humans and humanoids were merged together, creating the foundation of the energy system behind what later on became the LPRF3 galactic races in our LPU before the timeline event.

The genetic combination of the human-humanoids in the first universe were different from the other species and the merged races exhibited combinations of insectoid-humans, avian-humans, reptoid-humans and mammal-humans of which the mammal-humans were the highest developed races holding the peak consciousness genetics of the humanoids and the new consciousness traits of the humans.

The human-humanoids that chose to follow the Progenitors, i.e. the group of elder races that chose to split off from the first universe creating the less progressive universe (the LPU), mostly unfolded as participants of the Sirian Workstations on the LPRF3 galactic realities, whereas the humanoids chose to unfold in the LPRF2 stellar realities.

The reptoid-humans became the Maldakian races, which after the timeline event unfolded as the ancient Sirian Bs (a crossing between the LPRF2 stellar and LPRF3 galactic races) and the scattered LPRF3 galactic races. The mammal-humans and the mammal-humanoids that had followed the Progenitors became the galactic-stellar Sirian As, of which we know little since they vanished from our quadrant shortly after the ancient stellar races began to materialize their non-all-for-the-common-good mind-set.

Now with this in mind, we can return to the reptoid-humans or the Maldakian galactic races. The Maldakian galactic races were a mixed bunch; again the primitive traits that arose later from the regression in the stellar races had to have a type of dormant genetic predecessor and that came from the lesser developed genetic traits of the races that left the first universe. I´m not saying that they were primitive to begin with as they entered the LPU, only that they had areas of their reptoid genetics that were still in the process of developing from the individual level of things, viewing all from the perspective of I-AM and not from the all-for-the-common-good mind-set of the mammals.

The reptoid-humans were thus divided between the I-AM and the all-for-the-common-good mind-set as were all of the other LPU races struggling to develop their genetics to the high standard of the fifth evolutionary cycle and as we know; most of the humanoid races that entered the LPU had failed in this in the first universe and were now given a second chance in the LPU.

The humanoid-humans that followed, and became the LPRF3 galactic races, did so because of their higher ranked position in the Sirian Workstations, giving them the voice of leadership they had not gotten in the first universe, which were controlled by the humanoid elder races for all good reasons. In the time up until the split off, the elders had gained and incorporated the human consciousness more and more, leaving behind the humanoid consciousness traits and in this forgotten their ancestry and genetic soul groups still struggling to achieve the genetic consciousness features of the fifth evolutionary cycle.

In this the elder races and their human collaborators abandoned both the humanoid races and the merged races, which enabled the Progenitors to convince the humanoids and the human-humanoids to follow them into the LPU, where they would get a higher position in the overall evolutionary scheme of the LPU; the Progenitors elevated into pure consciousness (the LPRF5 beyond cosmic races) laying the foundation of the LPU, the central sun and the khundarays (implying that these items are the LPRF5s).

The LPRF3 galactic human-humanoids became the overseers of the evolutionary designs in the LPU and the lifeforms that were to unfold there, having the highest position in the LPU along with the principles of the 4th evolutionary cycle that had been given form in the LPU and from this turned into the LPRF4 cosmic races, i.e. the Elohim as they are called in the Hebrew Bible. The name refers to the Powers of Creation.

The Elohim were the highest lifeforms of the 4th evolutionary cycle that were more similar to principles than humanoids and they were, in an alliance with the galactic human-humanoid LPRF3s, to produce the light fields, i.e. the energy systems and gridworks from which all lifeforms would arise and into these seed the genetics from the first universe, creating new races and new realities.

The stellar LPRF2 humanoids were to unfold all forms of organic holographic features, using the created light fields of the Elohim-LPRF3s to their convenience following the holographic principles.

The LPRF2 stellar humanoids would unfold the various forms of semi-solid holographic realities into which their genetics could unfold, mature and develop. The holographic principles could only unfold when in use of the energy systems and gridworks of the collaborating Elohim-LPRF3s.

The LPRF2 stellar races were to work together across their racial genetic traits and in this progress the organic reality fields using the holographic units of the 4th evolutionary cycle as well as the principles of the Progenitors laid into the grids beneath their realities, fueled by the khundarays and upheld by the overseeing Elohim-LPRF3s.

The LPRF1 planetary races were the first real creation of the LPU, having the genetic set up of all the other four races, from the beyond cosmic LPRF5 races to the stellar LPRF2 humanoids.

In this we understand:
1) "Source" is the same as the LPRF5 beyond cosmic races unfolding as the central sun, the khundarays and the foundation of the LPU,

called the keys or origin of consciousness. The LPRF5s exist in a field of raw consciousness which includes the entire LPU from the lowest to the highest systems. The LPRF5s are to be found in all aspects of the LPU to a lesser or higher degree. The denser a LPU light field becomes, the fewer keys of consciousness it is able to hold and the farther away the connection to the LPRF5s is. Only if a human, a humanoid or a human-humanoid holds the keys can it connect to the raw consciousness of the LPRF5 and in this begin the true journey of ascension out of the LPU and back into the first universe.

2) The LPRF4-Elohim and the galactic LPRF3s were the beings of the highest and they worked together as a unit; that is the galactic LPRF3 human-humanoids expressed the consciousness of the LPRF4-Elohim and in this knew all that was to know regarding the principles of the 4th evolutionary cycle.

The combined LPRF4 principle-LPRF3 light human-humanoids were to oversee all lifeforms and reality fields in the LPU. They were the Founding Fathers of all human-humanoid races and the guardians of the humanoid stellar races. They existed before the timeline event as the major fields of light we today know as the cradles of life, i.e. as LPRF4 nebulae manifestations of extreme proportions and the LPRF3 galactic races unfolding as human-humanoids of considerable size, being considerably taller than other races and as such could dissolve into huge spheres of light or suns if they chose to do so.

The LPRF3 galactic human-humanoids had direct contact with the LPRF4 nebulae Elohim of which they were an extended manifestation or, to use another expression, incarnation.

A LPRF3 galactic human-humanoid was therefore in full contact with the highest forces of the LPU, its foundation and the mechanisms that created all forms of life.

The consciousness of an original LPRF3 unfolded on a galactic level, which leads us to the conclusion that the Sirian Workstation had the same size as a galaxy and perhaps was a galaxy.

3) After the timeline event the LPRF3 galactic races were detached from the LPRF4 Elohim and ceased to exist as an independent galactic race. They no longer existed in unity with the LPRF4 Elohim and thus lost their knowledge of the principles behind and controlling the 4th and 5th evolutionary cycles.

Most of the LPRF3 galactic races got trapped in the timeline loops of the timeline event, having their light fields and genetics scattered all over the timeline loops. Only the LPRF3s holding a high degree of mammal or human genetics could pull out becoming the galactic-stellar Sirian As and similar races that remained in contact with the LPRF4s and the LPRF5s and because of this continued to develop the original LPU beyond the repulsion barrier of the timeline event.

A small portion of the LPRF3s resurfaced as the ancient galactic-stellar Sirian Bs claiming to be the highest positioned races of our quadrant, i.e. the areas beyond the repulsion barrier, having lost the connection to the LPRF4 and LPRF5s. The ancient Sirian Bs took on the function as the new progenitors positioned in the higher councils, controlling the evolutions in the after timeline event LPU division.

A faction of the fragmented LPRF3s went into full degradation as light fields, being highly infected and in this separated further from the principles that had sustained their light fields. The highly infected LPRF3 light entities were quarantined in the LPF3 dark areas.[85]

Most of the scattered LPRF3s turned into light clusters consisting of merged energy systems and genetics stuck in the timeline loops.

---

[85] It has to be understood that the LPRF3 dark areas only look dark due to lack of quanta. The LPRF3s of that area still appear as light beings, albeit having a very cold form of light and their emission fields are similar to the properties of black holes.

These LPRF3 light clusters got trapped in the scattered light fields beneath the after timeline event LPU reality fields, having merged into these. However some of the LPRF3 light clusters attached, as a form of parasite, to the lower races and positioned themselves as a dormant consciousness and light aspect in energy systems of the stellar LPRF2s and planetary LPRF1s. Thus the LPRF3 light clusters became a participating aspect in the LOES of the LPRF1 and LPRF2 human-humanoids or humanoids.

The attached light element would here unfold the LPRF2 stellar genetics or the LPRF1 planetary genetics to new levels, although not as the genetics were supposed to following the inbuilt ascension abilities from before the timeline event. Instead the genetics would develop the attached LPRF3 light cluster into strands in the vortexes. The LPRF3 light clusters could in this merge their genetics with the genetics in the LOES vortexes and from there generate a merged type of consciousness, where the LPRF2 stellar humanoid or LPRF1 planetary human-humanoid slowly but surely changed into the LPRF3 human-humanoid, with portions of the original stellar or planetary consciousness intact.

The goal of this attachment was to gather genetics in as many timeline loops as possible, instructing the mind of the organic form (using the LOES and its vortexes as its intermediary energy system) how to perform the LPRF3 sciences. From this gathering the LPRF3 light cluster would be able to regenerate a functional LPRF3 light field able to generate a form in the realities controlled by the LPRF3s. The adapted organic form and the inbuilt LPRF3 consciousness would later on be called Avatars or Ascended Masters.

Instead of generating a LPRF3 human-humanoid form some of the LPRF3 light clusters would develop their light field to the highest level of consciousness using a lower racial entity with the purpose of overtaking the organic holographic form in full. In this process there would be no traces left of the original planetary or stellar personality. The goal was to develop the energy system and genetics into a LPRF3 galactic light field, transforming the lower holographic units into LPRF3 light units and from there gather as much of the original LPRF3 genetics from the timeline loops, using all means to do this. Such a fully transformed and restructured human-humanoid is called a Rishi.

Some of the scattered LPRF3s took on pure light forms using the leftovers of the LPRF4 principles and in this creating the light entities we find in realities in-between the LPU reality fields as well as the astral entities which unfolded on the astral plane, created by the infected LPRF3s, known to us as fairies, nature spirits, spiritual beings, guardians, angels, sprites etc. These LPRF3s had little of their original genetics left and thus unfolded as a new type of entities.

4) After the timeline event most of the LPRF1 planetary and LPRF2 stellar races changed from independent racial entities developing in their own image and rights into the function of healing and restoring the scattered or infected LPRF3s. The lower positioned LPRF1s and LPRF2s, in their full rights as a race, lost their independent ascension abilities, which had been an inbuilt right of all LPU races securing the four races of the LPU to be able to transit back into the first universe, if wanted.

The lower LPRF1 planetary and LPRF2 stellar races were re-created in the image of the LPRF3s, holding the LPRF3 genetics as part of their upper template or had incorporated LPRF3 light clusters containing larger portions of LPRF3 genetics and thus turned into an extension of these, where the LPRF3 genetics would slowly take over the LPRF1 planetary or LPRF2 stellar personality, partially or in full.

All in all the lower LPU races had lost their individual ascension abilities and were now to unfold all of their genetics into viable LOES fit to house the genetics of the LPRF3s, giving form and existence to them.

5) The timeline event has resulted in a full makeover of the reality fields on the LPRF1 planetary levels, where the particle realities were turned into an inner-outer type of realities with an outer solidified shell and inner realities holding the scattered and LPRF3 light fields, changing the holographic gridworks and thus the principles of the LPRF1 lifeforms. Therefore the gridwork and the racial networks are only part of the inner reality fields of our planet, i.e. the LPRF1 middle and upper levels and only the outer atomic levels are visible to us.

The LPRF2 stellar levels were turned into semi-solidified realities, albeit not having an inner-outer division but it changed the features of the original organic holographic worlds; also due to the scattered light fields.

The LPRF3 realities were demolished as an independent reality, leaving behind only the light fields as scattered bits and pieces captured in whirls of energy, constituting the galaxies we see today, having no lifeforms of their own.

The timeline event has prevented the races of this quadrant to complete the ascension process from the 4th to the 5th evolutionary cycle as it was set to unfold in the LPU.

After the timeline event the remaining LPRF3s took over the role of the progenitors in the majority of reality fields in our quadrant, making all of the races of our quadrant do their bidding.

The Puzzle of 7 Billion People

There have always been pieces of the puzzle I've had problems with fitting into the pattern of the prison planet scheme:

1. Why have the births of so many people been allowed since the 1700's when we know it literally kills the planet and thus the habitat of the remaining LPRF3s?
2. Why have all forms of sciences been allowed to flourish in our world since the 1700's? It would have been enough, in terms of astral energy production, to have the ancient emotional human type to produce the needed levels of astral energy.

To answer these questions we begin with the understanding that the manifested plane of reality, i.e. the planet itself, is uniform for all of the stellar races working here. The differences are to be found on the inner planes of existence upheld by the racial networks in the main gridwork. The inner planes of existence are the most important part of this planet and they are independent of the outer reality and at the same time they control it.

This goes back to the theories shown in *the Souls of Humanity* and *Terralogy* concerning the connection between the racial genetics belonging to the races in a reality field and their interaction with the grids of the planet. A race can only exist in a reality field if the racial genetics have been seeded into the gridwork of a reality field and in this generates a racial network. The racial network fuels the LOES via the heart vortex, whereas the quantum variables (QVs) from the core quantum fields (the CQFs) fuel the quantum morphogenetic field, i.e. the template of QVs and in this enables the LOES to create an organic holographic form in that reality field.

The main gridwork is first created as a light field, implementing the lines of the gridwork consisting of holographic units (fueled by the khundarays), which together becomes the template of the reality field. The template runs the principles of the field and what can be unfolded of lifeforms there. As such a reality field is a sort of entity composed of 4th evolutionary cycle holographic units and LPRF3 light units and it is linked to the LPRF4s, at least before the timeline event.

The idea of the LPRF5s were to alternate and transform the 4th evolutionary cycle units into 5th evolutionary cycle units built into the gridworks of the different reality fields existing in the LPRF1-LPRF3 systems providing the needed building blocks for the LPU races to eventually return to the first universe and the 5th evolutionary cycle of the first universe.

Unfortunately as our quadrant was altered by the timeline event, it impeded all the grand plans of the LPRF5s, at least in terms of our quadrant. This also had huge effects on our planet.

The outer manifested plane of our planet is equal to the original lower LPRF1 which to begin with was nothing more than fluctuating quantum fields, providing the LPRF1 non-solidified reality field with quantum variables (QVs) from the 3rd core quantum field (the CQF) made of units from the LPRF3 light field adapted to our LPRF1 system, QVs from the 2nd core quantum field made of LPRF2 holographic units adapted to our LPRF1 system, and the 1st core quantum field, enabling the original LPRF1 particles to unfold as organic-holographic matter based upon the main principles of the LPRF4s and the other LPRF races.

After the timeline event the 3rd CQF changed into a fragmented field of electromagnetic units with different frequencies instead of a pure unified field of LPRF3 light units. The 2nd CQF holographic units changed as well due to the new frequencies, producing a whole new type of particles, known to us as atomic particles based upon the four forces (the weak, the strong, the electromagnetic force and gravity). The atomic particles became the foundation of the manifested outer reality and the solidified version of the original particles, which turned the lower LPRF1 into a round planet.

The present day reality and its lifeforms had its beginning around 2500 BCE where our world changed from the lesser solidified levels that had been part of the reality which unfolded from the 26500 BCE take over by the LPRF2 human-humanoid Templars (the top of the LWBs) during the first fall.

The second fall, or change of our reality field, happened during the Reptilian Riots many thousand years ago that led to the takeover by the draco-reptilian overlords, pushing the Templars and their allied avian-mammal races into the position of the servile priesthood of the lizard landowners and in this formed the sub-ground resistance movement of the human-humanoid Templars called the left wing brotherhoods, plotting the plan of regaining the control of the LPRF1 reality field on all three levels.

The plan came into completion when the most functional of the infected LPRF3, from the quarantined LPRF3 areas, descended into our reality field, summoned by the lizard landowners and their dark priestly magic, invoking and bridging the antagonistic core of the LPR3 quarantined areas to our reality field in an attempt to gain more power and from this alter the outer reality by the use of the ancient sciences the quarantined LPRF3s held.

However the lizards did not have luck in controlling the invoked LPRF3 light entities because they were far more advanced than the lizards. Thus the infected, cold light LPRF3 entities came to our planet around 2500 BCE where they took over the LPRF1 upper levels and from there worked their way into the middle LPRF1 levels using the LOES of the Templars as their extended energy system. The Templars saw their chance of regaining what was lost during the Reptilian Riots with the incoming LPRF3s and in this offered their energy system to them, becoming one with the light fields of the scattered LPRF3s.

From there the LPRF3-Templars worked their way through the middle LPRF1 reality field controlled by the draco-reptilians and their affiliated reptoid-avian (dragon-moth and similar winged reptilian races being part of the Orion Collective), reptoid-insectoid (mantis and similar insectoid races, such as the tall Greys) and reptoid-mammal stellar races (Nordics, new Pleiadians, Arcturians etc).

The LPRF3-Templars negotiated treaties with the regressed stellar races that prior had collaborated with the draco-reptilians over the genetic gene pool this planet held in forms of dormant LOES from the time of the Templars, as well as the brought in LOES from other systems by the draco-reptilians using the lower LPRF1 area as a dumping ground for their enemies attaching the sealed off LOES to a worker form, i.e. the outer human population.

As we know the lizard landowners (the bloodlines) functioned as kings, rulers and landowners and as the draco-reptilians were pushed out by the more intelligent and advanced cold light LPRF3-Templars, when in form as human-humanoids, the lizards changed side as they always do and became the controllers of the manifested outer reality.

The new planetary reality arose as a result of the astral plane and astral barrier, engineered by advanced LPRF3 technologies. The astral barrier and astral plane were attached to the ancient crystal pillar technologies, forgotten by the draco-reptilians, but also seeded as consciousness into the LPRF1 gridwork by the use of infected LPRF3 genetics into the existing LPRF3 network. The ancient LPRF3 network had been seeded for a purpose of ascension possibilities granted to the LPRF1s and later on it was modified to the sustain the restoration programs of the colonies and in this already holding the distortion as a sub-program set to heal it. The LPRF3-Templars changed all of this to create the new reality fitting their new program.

The outer human population was changed energetically to fit the energetic requirements of the cold LPRF3s who had now taken over the entire LPRF1 system, including what we call the solar system.

112

The outer human population got a chakra system controlling their thoughts and emotions to fit the necessities of the type of astral energy the cold light LPRF3s needed as well as producing the lower astral forms of energy needed to feed the lesser functional LPRF3s, now having a new home in the middle LPRF1 areas, called the astral plane.

The lesser functional LPRF3s had not survived the quarantine well and had dissolved into small amounts of LPRF3 genetics. Because of this they were unable to uphold an energy system. In their new home on the astral plane, the lesser functional LPRF3s became the nature forces, called devas in new age, in higher forms and as the sprites in minor forms; all infected and emitting the cold light signature.

The devas in our reality field are therefore to be seen as the astral version of a LPRF3 human-humanoids, having taken on a form using the astral energies and in this turned into the leading principle of the astral plane; calling themselves kings and queens and not the 4th root race. Hence all magic have to addresses the high lords of the four corners, asking the astral LPRF3s for permission to do energy work on the astral plane (only a brotherhood prerogative).

At the same time the LPRF2 stellar humanoids , that stayed behind and collaborated with the cold light LPRF3s, and the Templar human-humanoids, i.e. the highest ranked LWBs slowly but surely were taken over by the LPRF3s acting as their masters. From this cooperation the LPRF2 stellar humanoids and planetary human-humanoid LWBs were sucked dry of quanta, generating a field of darkness in them.

This naturally accelerated the need for viable genetics and quanta in the LPRF3s, the LWBs and the darkened LPRF2s humanoids, and new means of advancement in the energy production - provided by the outer humanity - were taken to provide an upgrade for the LPRF3s that fed of their affiliated LPRF2s and the darkened LWBs.

This is when outer humanity leaves the dark Middle Ages. At that point the Templar-LWBs had turned so dark that not even the higher positioned LPRF3s could feed of them anymore. Instead the LPRF3s had begun to merge with the regressed and darkened LWBs turning into the LPRF2 dark masters we know of today, only able to exist on the astral plane.

The other LPRF3s were forced to prey on the dark antagonistic core and in this depleting the remnants of the LPRF3 gridwork still present in the quarantined areas of the destroyed LPRF3 system as well as the planetary LPRF3 network, which together in the end would destroy the LPRF3s. At the same time the astral plane and the astral barrier sunk into lower and lower frequencies adding chaos to all planes of existence in the LPRF1.

In this chaos the lizard landowners, still having their LOES intact and getting their QVs from their own racial networks, regained more control and new attempts were made to invite back in the forces of the draco-reptilian overlords. Only a minor faction of the overlords came in, and in this gained support from some factions of the LWBs; dividing the LWBs under the Templars and the draco-reptilians.

The outer functioning LWBs (as popes and bishops; i.e. outer humans with an activated Templar-LWB LOES) tried to control the landowners through the means of religion, instigating severe religious control and other forms of power plays but the landowners retaliated by inserting their bought and selected priests and clerks (having no formal education as priests or clerks, being nobilities themselves) into their land districts circumventing the main control of Rome. Thus new levels of intelligence were the solution, giving more juice to the human population and through this diminish the power of the landowners and their affiliated draco-reptilian overlords.

In the last parts of the 1700's new sciences were inserted into the astral barrier to enable humanity to produce a higher type of energy called mental energy. This secured the existence of the cold light LPRF3s in the middle LPRF1 areas and reestablished the energies of the inner LWBs, enabling them to function in their semi-holographic forms by the use of the mental energies and plane.

The astral energies were pushed a back into their original position in the lower levels of the middle LPRF1 areas.

New education systems were inserted teaching the outer humans to work with their mind and from this produce a higher quality of chakras, which were able to function as an extension for the LPRF2 dormant LOES and in this assure the needed quanta production for the LPRF3s.

A side gain was that the LPRF3s were now able to work in the lower LPRF1 areas, using the dormant LPRF2 LOES attached to the upgraded chakra system. By doing this they regained the power over the lizard controllers that kind of had gone way beyond their jurisdiction during the Middle Ages in their search for more power and property.

The LPRF3s did not regain power over the landowners that again were under the overlords and treaties were made between the factions; however as we know this LWB faction and their affiliated lizards and draco-reptilian overlords and warriors, i.e. the Illuminati, went to America and created the first version of the New Order of the Ages (the NOA). Order was reestablished around the old world giving back the control of the LPRF1 to the cold light LPRF3s.

Before, the LPRF3s had relied on the Templar-LWBs but due to the new circumstances some of the LPRF3s incarnated directly using the new energy systems and more dormant LOES were pulled in from the hidings of the brotherhoods to ensure quality LOES for the LPRF3s.

The incarnating LPRF3s became the highest level of power in the LWB hierarchy, pushing the Templar-LWBs a nudge down (now calling themselves the Ascended Masters) as well as the dark LPRF2s into a defined and enclosed section on the astral plane. This forced the some of the Templar-LWBs to take on positions in the outer realty on all levels of society, posing as a control mechanism for the nobilities, i.e. the landowners and presiding over the new teaching, societal and economic systems, which had arisen from the upgrading of the astral barrier.

At the same time more outer or worker humans were produced to ensure the correct level of mental energies, enabling the LPRF3s and LPRF2s to build new planes of existence. In this the human population rose to new heights and this have not ended, considering the new plans of the LPRF3s, which includes affiliations with the crystalline Sirian Bs.

This should answer the questions:
1. Why have the births of so many people been allowed since the 1700's when we know it literally kills the planet and thus the habitat of the remaining LPRF3s?
2. Why have all forms of sciences been allowed to flourish in our world since the 1700's? It would have been enough, in terms of astral energy production, to have the ancient emotional human type to produce the needed levels of astral energy.

Lightning Source UK Ltd.
Milton Keynes UK
UKHW020633200622
404682UK00008B/181